WICKED
GOOD WORDS

ALSO BY MIM HARRISON

Smart Words
Words at Work

WICKED GOOD WORDS

From Johnnycakes to Jug Handles,
a Roundup of America's Regionalisms

Mim Harrison

PERIGEE BOOKS
A Stonesong Press Book

A PERIGEE BOOK
Published by the Penguin Group
Penguin Group (USA) Inc.
375 Hudson Street, New York, New York 10014, USA

Penguin Group (Canada), 90 Eglinton Avenue East, Suite 700, Toronto, Ontario
M4P 2Y3, Canada (a division of Pearson Penguin Canada Inc.) • Penguin Books
Ltd., 80 Strand, London WC2R 0RL, England • Penguin Group Ireland,
25 St. Stephen's Green, Dublin 2, Ireland (a division of Penguin Books Ltd.) •
Penguin Group (Australia), 250 Camberwell Road, Camberwell, Victoria 3124,
Australia (a division of Pearson Australia Group Pty. Ltd.) • Penguin Books
India Pvt. Ltd., 11 Community Centre, Panchsheel Park, New Delhi—110 017,
India • Penguin Group (NZ), 67 Apollo Drive, Rosedale, Auckland 0632,
New Zealand (a division of Pearson New Zealand Ltd.) • Penguin Books
(South Africa) (Pty.) Ltd., 24 Sturdee Avenue, Rosebank, Johannesburg 2196,
South Africa

Penguin Books Ltd., Registered Offices: 80 Strand, London WC2R 0RL, England

Copyright © 2011 by Mim Harrison and the Stonesong Press LLC
Text design by Laura K. Corless

First edition: August 2011

Library of Congress Cataloging-in-Publication Data

Harrison, Mim, 1955–
   Wicked good words : from johnnycakes to jug handles, a roundup of America's
regionalisms / Mim Harrison.— 1st ed.
   p.   cm.
   "A Stonesong Press Book."
   Includes bibliographical references and index.
   ISBN 978-0-399-53676-2
   1. Americanisms. 2. English language—United States—Usage. 3. English
language—United States—Idioms. I. Title.
   PE2835.H37   2011
   427'.973—dc22   2011010318

PRINTED IN THE UNITED STATES OF AMERICA

10 9 8 7 6 5 4 3 2

For Nigel.
Who ever else?

And for Heather,
with love and admiration.

CONTENTS

INTRODUCTION

The idea of geography as destiny has long been embedded in the American character. We say what we do in part because of where we live and where we grew up. Technology was supposed to change this; national television, in particular, was going to strip the country of its regional ways.

It hasn't happened.

We may all eat at the same chain restaurants, drink the same brands of coffee, shop at the same stores, carry the same iPhones—but we still talk like we're from somewhere in particular. Maybe not as much as we once did, but we can still give ourselves away geographically through what we say. And that's just the way we like it.

Beg, Borrow, Steal—Deal!

When you consider where we came from linguistically, you realize that it's practically in the genetic code of Americans' primary language to take on the trappings of its surroundings. English is both wonderfully adaptive and stubbornly resilient—just the combination you need to generate regional expressions that stick.

After all, could there be a language more willing to borrow (beg or steal) from other languages than English? No wonder it's so tough for nonnative speakers to figure it out. As the writer Melvyn Bragg observes, it is the language's "most subtle and ruthless characteristic of all: its capacity to absorb others."

What began in the way-back machine as a Germanic tongue soon annexed a fair amount of Latin and, through it, some Greek. The precedent was set, and the Norman conquest of England in 1066 clinched it: all comers, welcome or not, would be considered as far as words that would be adopted into English. English is the great sponge of other languages, absorbing what works for it in a most equal-opportunity—albeit often random—of ways. Beggars, as they say, can't be choosers, and there is an advantage of not being so.

If by chance English speakers needed a word they couldn't find in what passed for the dictionaries of the day, they simply made one up. A certain playwright named William Shakespeare was famous for that. He either invented or imported into his repertoire of English more than two thousand new words, from "barefaced" to "leap-frog" and "horrid" to "vast." It was shortly after Big Will helped to reinvent and reinvigorate the English language, making it more colorful, more dramatic—and more wordy—that some of the English people said, "Check, please," and sailed off for America. The stage was set and the seeds sown for the English colonists—soon to be the Americans—to have a rich harvest in terms of their language.

The Puritans might not have had religious freedom where they came from, but they did have a language that knew how to borrow freely. And they might have been rigid when it came to their religion, but they did know how to bend, if only a little, to their surroundings when it came to their language.

The Dictionary as Tool of Revolution

The *Mayflower* English with their English language were not, by any stretch, the first to arrive in America. The Spanish were already here, as were some French, as well as the Dutch along the Hudson, and, of course, the Native Americans. The combination meant that soon an American language would become the great regionalism of English. (Even today, Americans toss things in a garbage can while the English use a dustbin.) Some of these new "regionalisms" were a result of what the immigrants saw around them that they had never seen before—a "crevasse," a "groundhog," a "possum."

But an American way of speaking was not initially embraced or desired, even by the most patriotic of the bunch. The country's Founding Fathers turned to a most English of dictionaries to hone the language of our nation's cherished documents of freedom—the Declaration of Independence, the Constitution, the Bill of Rights. The dictionary of English that the great and grumpy lexicographer Samuel Johnson published in 1755 was the go-to guide of the language for the learned on both sides of the Pond.

Johnson was an Englishman who would always be in England—more specifically, in London. "When a man is tired of London," he famously proclaimed, "he is tired of life." He was no fan of the colonies and made no secret of his distaste for Americans. He especially despised the slavery that was rampant in parts of the colonies. (Both George Washington and Thomas Jefferson owned a Johnson dictionary.) In 1756 Johnson was the first to make reference—dismissively, no doubt—to an "American dialect."

English Earns Its Stars and Stripes

Ironically, Samuel Johnson became the unwitting poster child of the malleability and porousness of the English language—the very qualities a language needs to steep itself in regionalisms. When he set out in 1747 to write a comprehensive dictionary of English, he was determined to tame the unruliness of the language. The French, after all, had an academy whose job was to keep its tongue in check. English needed a similar straitjacket.

Eight long, exhausting years later, when Johnson finally published his dictionary on April 15, 1755, he had abandoned all ideas of ever getting English to button up, stop wiggling, stay still, and cease changing. In fact, he applauded those very qualities, stating in the preface to his dictionary: "Every increase of knowledge, whether real or fancied, will produce new words."

Perhaps no American has been more keen to prove that maxim than Noah Webster. He made Americans stop spelling certain words the way the English did—who needed that *u* in "honor" and "color"? But he also defined and spotlighted the new words of a new land: "tomato," "prairie," "noodle." His point, ably brought home in *An American Dictionary of the English Language* in 1828, was, "If local terms exist, why not explain them?"

Webster stuck to single words rather than expressions, but he was clearly on to something close to regionalisms with his idea of "local terms."

The Ever-Mobile American Language

That first wave of English from England was just that: the first. Many more people and their words would come—not just English from other parts of England, but also the Scots, Irish, Germans, French Canadians, Spaniards, West Africans, Scandinavians, and Asians from the west.

They would settle in other parts of the country. Some would stay there forever; others would stay for a while and then go farther afield. Events such as the California Gold Rush would trigger a new wave of movement whose ripples would be felt far beyond California.

Like the language, those speaking it and learning it would not stop wiggling, stay still, or cease changing. Where New Americans went, so went their way of viewing the world, perspectives that shine through in our often colorful and sometimes curious expressions.

Okay, but Do You Really Talk Like This?

It's not surprising, then, that many of our local idioms are a reflection of who we've been, how we got here, and the way we might make our living. What you'll find in this book is a sampling of how locals speak now *and* how we used to talk. These words give us a sense of a region's past as well as present. If you're a New Englander, you might be all too familiar with nor'easters but not know about mooncussers. If you're a Californian, you might know the meaning of "piker" but not be aware of your state's role in coining the term.

This harking back to our histories is one reason why a near-vanishing way of speaking, such as Pennsylvania Dutch or Gullah or Bonac, still tugs at language lovers' hearts. As individuals, these expressions may not be our heritage. As a country, they are.

Some of these words are antiques, or on their way to being such. But before we shove them in the attic, they just might be worth rediscovering. They will plant you in a place that much more deeply.

Whether they be old or new, the expressions gathered in this book are a way to make you feel more at home in places you've never been. Utter "uff da" at the right moment to a Minnesotan, ask a New Orleans bartender for a "go-cup," say "geoduck" the way they do in Seattle, and no matter where you're from, you're home. (Well, sort of. Hey, it's a start.)

Those Devilsome Dialects

Rather than digressing into dialects—those accents that we're always surprised to hear we have—*Wicked Good Words* focuses on expressions. Start talking dialects and the discussion becomes fraught with linguistic terms such as fricatives, back vowel fronting, double modals, unglided vowels, and other eye-glazing-over terms. It's enough to give most of us the weary dismals, as they say in Tennessee. We'll leave relexifying and decreolization to another book, and stick with words in this one.

"But You Left Out This Word"

Among the fears and trepidations in writing about how Americans speak is knowing that you'll never capture all of the expressions—unless you're the brave souls who created the *Dictionary of American Regional English* (the acronym, DARE, is apt). But they required five hefty volumes to do it.

So if your favorite bit of local lingo is missing from

Wicked Good Words, please tell me of my wicked ways in overlooking it. Just visit my blog at http://mimharrison.com and post a comment.

One last note: a reader from, say, the East might puzzle over why certain words ended up in the chapters to the west ("spider" is one such). When Americans migrate, so does their language. Certain terms end up being more at home in their new home than their old. Thus the newly arrived eventually become the locals.

All politics is local, said Tip O'Neill famously (with his famously thick Boston accent). It turns out language is, too. Language and weather are two of the most enduring differences that unite us. May it always be so.

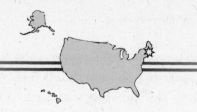

WICKED PISSA

New England

The European ancestors of these folks got here before almost everybody else, so New Englanders are allowed to talk funny. Their roots in England run deep, although settlers from lots of other countries later joined them (think of the Irish who came to Boston). And try as they might, they've never totally lost that Puritan ethic. This is still the place where you'll find drawer space reserved for pieces of string too small to save.

American chop suey. Ground beef and macaroni in a tomato sauce. Go to many a casual restaurant in New England, including River's Edge Café in downtown Wakefield, Rhode Island, and you'll find this delightful contradiction of terms. What could possibly be American about a dish whose name is more closely associated with bean sprouts and water chestnuts? Traditional chop suey is a mix of Chinese veggies and chicken or pork, but you won't find a dish called chop suey in China, either. The term may date back to the early 1880s, when American ears first misheard the Cantonese word *tsapsui*, meaning a mixture. So why not make an America version of this Americanized term, using burger and pasta? As one Rhode Islander put it, American chop suey is Hamburger Helper before there was such a thing.

banker. Not the shirt-and-tie variety, but a commercial fisherman who fishes the Grand Banks off of Newfoundland. Sometimes, though not always, after one of these trips he smiles all the way to the bank.

the Big Ditch. Anglers know it well, and don't worry, you can't just fall into it. The Big Ditch is the Cape Cod Canal, the man-made waterway that separates the Cape from the mainland of Massachusetts. It makes the Cape, in effect, an island, although nobody ever says so. The Big Ditch was dug twice—first by a private financier in 1914, when it was more like the Little Ditch, then again in the 1930s by the U.S. government. Fishermen most likely gave it its name. Up the road a piece in Boston, they recently undertook a similar large-scale project, this time on land. It was known officially as the Central Artery Tunnel Project. The locals just call it the **Big Dig**.

cleanser. Not the kind that cleans your face but the kind that cleans your clothes. This version of "dry cleaner," first recorded in 1958, is seen in written form more than it is heard and spoken. Where there's "tonic" (see page 79), there's "cleanser": look for the term primarily in the Boston area.

cold roast Boston. If it sounds like a leftover Sunday roast that's served cold the next day by staunchly conservative Bostonians, it is—sort of. It's the name that Ralph Waldo Emerson's brother-in-law, Thomas Gold Appleton (1812–84), conferred on a particular breed of Bostonian also known as the **Boston Brahmin**. These are the elite WASPs of the city and descendants of its founders. Oliver Wendell Holmes Sr., himself a Brahmin, coined "Boston Brahmin" in an 1860 article in the *Atlantic Monthly*. (He also later eulogized Appleton in the magazine.) The memorable poem by someone nobody remembers (not a Brahmin) captures the essence of the cold roast Boston:

And this is good old Boston
The home of the bean and the cod,
Where the Lowells talk to the Cabots,
And the Cabots talk only to God.

"She's cold roast Boston" is the kind of thing you'd say in confidence—and only to someone who wasn't.

common. Elsewhere it may be known as a park or a square, but in Boston in particular, it's a common. Thus Boston Common is the large public park that's a centerpiece of the city. And no, it's not "commons," even though that may sound more natural (to non-Bostonians). The term goes back to the beginnings of Boston and New England. A common is a public space available to all, both man and beast—cows grazed here till 1830. The word was being used in similar ways in England as far back as Chaucer in the 1300s. People did hang in Boston Common way back when, but not quite the way they do now. The Common is where public hangings took place until 1817.

cracky benders. Making a game out of running and sliding on ice that's thin enough that it just might crack. This is an old sport in Connecticut; the rest of us first heard about it in 1943. In Pennsylvania, the same kind of ice is sometimes called **kittly-bender**.

they crawling good? The proper way to ask a Maine lobsterman if he's catching any lobster—because his catch crawls on the ocean floor.

down the Cape. Heading toward Provincetown, the tip of Cape Cod, Massachusetts. It sounds straightforward enough till you check the map. About midway down the Cape, where the "elbow" bends, the land takes a northerly turn: it points *up*. A Bostonian explained with a perfectly straight face why you are nevertheless still going *down* the Cape even if you are traveling north: anytime you're going farther away from Boston, you're going down. If that's a hard one to swallow, try the anatomy lesson explanation. Back to that Cape "elbow": the land mass before the elbow is equivalent to your upper arm and shoulder. The land mass after the elbow is like your lower arm and fist. So if you're traversing the lower part of your arm, you're going down. Thoreau got into the whole arm-and-elbow thing when he traveled down the Cape in the 1850s:

> *Cape Cod is the bared and bended arm of Massachusetts: the shoulder is at Buzzard's Bay; the elbow, or crazy-bone, at Cape Mallebarre; the wrist at Truro; and the sandy fist at Provincetown.*

Down-Easter. One who's a native of up-yonder Maine. What's up with the "down" for this northern state—a case of a compass gone awry? No, just those Bostonians again and their geography. "Down-East" is old nautical terminology, from when ships sailed out of Boston toward Maine on a northeasterly wind. Oliver Wendell Holmes talked about going "down East" back in 1861.

dropped egg. A poached egg—because you drop it in water in order to poach it. But don't try ordering this unless you're in New England, or you might have egg on more than your face. You can find instructions on how to make a dropped egg in the classic New England collection of recipes called *The Boston Cooking-School Cook Book*, first published in 1896. You may know it by its other name: *The Fannie Farmer Cookbook*. Here's Ms. Farmer's 1918 recipe for the proper way to drop eggs:

> *Have ready a frying-pan two-thirds full of boiling salted water, allowing one-half tablespoon salt to one quart of water. Put two or three buttered muffin rings in the water. Break each egg separately into a saucer, and carefully slip into a muffin ring. The water should cover the eggs. When there is a film over the top, and the white is firm, carefully remove with a buttered skimmer to circular pieces of buttered toast. . . .*

fence viewer. The local official who regulates fences. Doesn't every town have one? Actually, the job has pretty much gone the way of the buggy whip, but back in the day when fences were an important way of defining property, the fence viewer was a busy fellow. He was primarily in New England, although the term has been recorded as early as 1657 in Long Island. Nowadays the expression is little used but deserves a revival, as it's the ideal metaphor to describe the person who doesn't do much but still has a title. Nice work if you can get it.

frog run of the sap. The last batch of maple syrup you're apt to get for the season. Maple sap is collected for syrup in the very early spring, before the frogs appear. A comparable expression is **bud run of the sap**, meaning the trees are in bloom so spring is in full swing—and no more sap will be flowing. Frogs figure prominently in Southern-speak (see FINE AS FROG'S HAIR and FROG STRANGLER), but this particular frog is a Vermonter. The term was first recorded in 1947 but probably used long before then. "This bucket has the frog run of the sap," you might hear the Vermonter say, "so enjoy the last of the syrup till next year."

fub around. Waste time, futz, fritter away the day. You hear it mainly in Maine, where historically the traditionally industrious Yankees don't do much fubbing. But somebody must have been doing just that back in 1902, because that's when the term was recorded. Along with wasting time, "fub" also suggests a lack of activity, as in the newer term "futz," which might be connected to the German *furzen*: to fart. Those who futz and fub can also be said to fart around.

gaumy. Clumsy when you're in northern New England, most notably in Maine. It works as both an adjective ("he's WICKED gaumy with those big feet") and a noun ("he's some gaumy the way he trips over his own toes"). "Gaumy" hails from *gom*, a noun the Irish were familiar with back at least as far as the 1830s. The word started out as the Irish *gamal*, meaning a simpleton—a poor awkward clod of a fellow.

get your bait back. Break even. If you're a commercial fisherman, one way to break even is to pay for your bait.

gurrybutt. Next time you serve clams or mussels or lobster and put a bowl on the table to collect the empty shells, impress your guests by suggesting they put their discards in the gurrybutt. "Gurry" is an old whaling term for fish offal. Even Rudyard Kipling knew the word; he used it in *Captains Courageous*, his 1897 novel about the Grand Banks. Kipling did part of his research for the book in the Massachusetts fishing village of Gloucester.

hit the felt. Hit the hay, in Maine paper-mill parlance— in other words, go to bed. Paper-making machines have a heavy felt blanket that contains the wet pulp. When it wears out its usefulness on the machine, it can be trimmed into blankets for beds.

ice-cream shot. An easy shot (and nothing like a Jell-O shot). The expression dates back to the days when ice cream was brought to Maine hunting camps in big tubs, and the salt and ice it was packed in was dumped in a designated spot. The salt attracted the deer, so shooting one while it licked the salt was a no-brainer: an ice-cream shot.

just 'cause your cat has kittens in the oven don't make 'em biscuits. Just because you've lived in Maine since you were an hour old, that doesn't make you a native. (Read the "don't" in the expression as "doesn't.") Okay, maybe that's an exaggeration, but not by much. No matter that those first European settlers were themselves *arrivistes*—unless you're born in New England, you'll never be a full-fledged New Englander. (You can move there and live there for years and still be considered a transient.) Even if your kids are born there but you weren't, there's some question as to whether "native" really applies to them.

killhag. A trap for catching various animals. You're likely to hear the word in Maine and New Hampshire, and it's an oldie—since 1784. Its origin is even older than that, as the word is rooted in the Algonquian for "catch."

like pigs on ice. Very slippery. Pigs don't walk on ice— they slither and skate on it.

like salts through a goose. Anything that happens like this happens extremely quickly. Geese are not known for being constipated. Compound that with medicinal salts that act as a purgative, and you have one quick trip. "My paycheck disappeared so fast, it was like salts through a goose."

the luck of Hiram Smith. Luckless in the extreme. Exceedingly unlucky Hiram was the only soldier to die in the Aroostook War of 1836–39, the tussle between the United States and England over Maine's northern border. The irony is that nary a shot was fired in this war, but Hiram managed to die anyway—because of either an illness or a freak accident. "First his car was stolen, then his bike, then his shoes. He has the luck of Hiram Smith."

mackerel sky. A cloud-streaked sky in New England. You're most likely to hear the phrase among the old salts (longtime sailors). The expression harks back to the mid- to late seventeenth century, and it's really no surprise that people who lived with the sea used a fishing metaphor. The markings on the Atlantic mackerel resemble streaks of clouds, at least to a fisherman's eye. **"Two days wet and one day dry"** goes the rhyme about the mackerel sky; when you see such a sky, expect it to rain.

minge. A gnat, or what's often called a midge. The word has been flying around since 1895; the gnats/minges/midges/no-see-ums have been flying around Maine and New Hampshire a lot longer than that.

mooncusser. We could say "one who cusses at the moon" and leave it at that, or we could spin the old New England yarn about the scavengers of shipwrecks (who no doubt caused some of them) who cursed the moon. These wreckers would shine lantern lights from the shore at night, to try to confuse the ships and lure them in. But if the moon was up, exposing the shore—and the men on it—so was their jig. A mooncusser, then, was a scavenger caught in the act. This was an old term even when it appeared in the *Old Farmer's Almanac* for 1813, and doesn't get much use anymore. But it's a good tale to tell the next time you're out at night and the moon shines bright.

New York system. A hot dog served only in Rhode Island. Actually, don't even call it a hot dog: this one's a wiener. The name "New York system" was adopted by the Greek restaurateurs of the early 1900s who left the environs of the Big Apple and moved to Little Rhody. They figured the moniker would give their wieners more credibility. Something worked, because these wieners-with-the-works are an institution in many parts of the state. You start with a small wiener in a bun, add mustard, meat sauce with secret ingredients, and then onions. Here's the clincher: the authentic way for the chefs to add the condiments is to line up a small battalion of the wieners—on their arms.

nor'easter. A three-day blow, or storm, that sometimes hangs around for five. "Northeaster" was recorded as early as 1774. But even the literary *Atlantic Monthly* had dropped the *th* by 1865—perhaps because the magazine's founders were New Englanders who'd grown up getting drenched by these wet, chill winds.

numb as a hake. Dumb as a doorknob, in Maine–New Hampshire speak. In other words, quite slow and bordering on stupid. You can also say just "numb as hake," the syllabic equivalent of "dumb as s——." But "numb" is a somewhat softer insult than "dumb." Hake is a kind of cod, and it seems to be getting a bad rap here, as it's no number or dumber than other fish. Perhaps it was just in the wrong New England waters at the wrong time. Interestingly, in the 1880s, "numb" was a noun rather than an adjective. According to the *Oxford English Dictionary*, it meant "a cold which numbs fish." And since at least the 1800s, "numb" has suggested ineptitude. Think of "numbheaded" (1850s), "numbskull" (1940s), "numb nuts" (1960s). Local sighting: the signs advertising an insurance company called Unum have been known to have "as a hake" mysteriously appended to them.

oakum, as in "I put the oakum on him." It means you shut him up but good. Oakum is a tarred hemp mixture used to shut up, or seal, the seams in boats.

off-islander. A thinly veiled code for one who is an outsider to Nantucket. This Nantucketism was first heard in the 1880s, probably by one who was such a person. Unless you're a native, you're an off-islander even when you're on this island. In *Nantucket: A History* (1914), the author gives two examples of "off-islander":

> *A Nantucket schoolboy being asked to mention the situation of Alaska, located it as being "in the northwest corner of off-island."* . . . *Another began a composition thus: "Napoleon was a great man; he was a great soldier and a great statesman—but he was an off-islander!"*

Old Ironsides. The affectionate nickname of the USS *Constitution*, a three-masted frigate and the country's oldest warship still afloat. She's moored in the Charlestown Navy Yard in Boston, still basking in the glory of her heroics in the War of 1812, when she shrugged off repeated assaults by the British. One of the sailors declared her sides to be made of iron. (She's a wooden ship.) Oliver Wendell Holmes's 1830 poem "Old Ironsides" saved the *Constitution* from the scrap heap, an early example of historic preservation.

package store. Where New Englanders buy their booze, even though much of the rest of the country goes to a liquor store. The term is a relic of post-Prohibition days, when stalwart souls still didn't care to associate with the likes of boozy-sounding words. "Package" most likely suggests the (usually plain) paper bag you get at checkout. So when New Englanders make a **packie run**, they're going to the liquor store.

potato bargain. A stew of onion, pork, and potatoes, the recipe for which you can get in the 1939 *New England Yankee Cook Book*. These ingredients add up to a cheap meal in New England, so it's a bargain.

rawny. Raw-boned, in the sense of big-boned. Think of brawny and you're just about there. It's a word that's been around since at least the 1860s.

red flannel hash. Corned-beef hash with beets, which make it red. The **red-hash supper** first appeared in print in 1907 but was no doubt on the plates of waste-not New Englanders well before that. A 1939 cookbook pegged it as the encore performance of the New England boiled dinner, a way to use up the leftover meat and vegetables, spruced up with the beets. That's in keeping with the New England credo of **"use it up, wear it out, make it do, or do without."**

Native Sum

The first book to be published in America was the Bay Psalm Book, in 1640. It was printed in English. The first Bible in America was published in 1663. It was printed in Algonquian. A Puritan pastor named John Eliot translated the Bible from English to this indigenous tongue. Granted, the point of the printing was to win converts among the Native Americans; nevertheless, the New Americans were already demonstrating that they had an ear for their surroundings.

While the country's new arrivals didn't immediately adopt a slew of Native American terms, they did borrow a number of them. In some ways no words are more regional than these. They defined America's surroundings in ways no other words could, and they described things not seen outside America.

- That four-legged creature with the black-rimmed eyes was a *raughroughouns*, or *aracouns*, soon to be shortened even further to the more pronounceable *raccoon*.
- The creature that literally raised a stink when cornered was a *segankn*, or *skunk*.
- That good-tasting gourd (once you figured out how to cook it) was *isquontersquash*—or *squash*, for short.

> *Pecan, persimmon, chipmunk, moose, barbecue, hominy, toboggan, kayak, mugwump*—all of these have roots in the indigenous languages of the Americas. As settlers ventured ever farther west in the 1800s, they became ever more attuned to the local languages: in their journals, Lewis and Clark recorded five hundred Native American terms as they made their way west from Saint Louis to the Pacific coast in 1804.

scrod. The short definition is: fish. Depending on where you look up the word, you can get two very different senses of it:

Urban Dictionary: "The past passive pluperfect [*sic*] of 'to screw.'"
Merriam-Webster Online: "Past participle of *scraw*"—meaning to split and dry young fish.

Let's put it this way: some people who order scrod at a restaurant or fish market might feel they've gotten screwed. Scrod is like the fishy version of mystery meat. It could be cod, perhaps it's haddock, possibly pollock, and most likely it's whatever was the cheapest catch of that day. People have been getting scrod since the 1800s. When you see scrod on a menu, it's advisable to ask what it is. Just be careful how you ask. And it's best not to say, "I feel like getting scrod tonight."

TEST YOUR I.L.Q.—INDIGENOUS LANGUAGE QUOTIENT

Only two of the original thirteen states have names that draw from the indigenous languages. Can you guess which ones?

> **ANSWER:** They are Connecticut ("at the long tidal river") and Massachusetts ("near the small big mountain").

Indigenous names for territories (and eventually states) picked up steam as American settlers went west. How many states in total have names rooted in indigenous languages?

> **ANSWER:** Just over half of them. They are:

Alabama	Mississippi
Alaska	Missouri
Arizona	Nebraska
Arkansas	New Mexico
Connecticut	North Dakota
Idaho	Ohio
Illinois	Oklahoma
Iowa	South Dakota
Kansas	Tennessee
Kentucky	Texas
Massachusetts	Utah
Michigan	Wisconsin
Minnesota	Wyoming

Although Washington, DC, doesn't make this list, the name of its river, the Potomac, is from the Algonquian.

"See a sea glin, catch a wet skin." A red-sky/weather kind of rhyme. "Glin" is "glint," the light on the horizon in cold weather that signals bad weather is on the way— much the way a red sky in the morning is the sailor's warning that unsettled weather is ahead.

spa. The drugstore, but only in Boston and environs. More precisely, the "soda fountain," in the old-fashioned sense of the word (see page 80). The spa was the place where one went to partake of carbonated drinks, which were inspired by the mineral water from springs like those in Spa, Belgium. Today there are few such places left, but one that hangs on in Boston is Hillside Spa Cardoza Brothers.

Swamp Yankee. Legend has it that during the American Revolution, a group of Connecticut residents fled to the swamps in order to avoid an attack by the British. But the term has gone far beyond the legend to mean descendants of those early settlers who are known for being stoic, stubborn, frugal, and hardworking, unwilling to suffer fools or most politicians, and fiercely independent. Connecticut is the number one place for Swamp Yankees, with parts of Rhode Island—notably South County—coming in second. Is the term an insult or a compliment? That depends. Let's just say that if you're not a Swamp Yankee, it's probably best not to use the term.

All Shook Up over Milk Shakes

In Rhode Island, as in other parts of New England, the locals know "milk shake" to mean nothing but milk shaken up with some syrup. If there's ice cream involved, it's not a milk shake in Rhode Island: it's a **cabinet**. The pharmacist who first concocted it kept either the ice cream or the mixer in a cabinet, which is how the ice cream–based milk shake got its unexpected name.

Hop the border into Massachusetts and the cabinet turns into a **frappe**—from the French *frapper*, meaning "to ice." In other parts of New England, the frappe is a **velvet**. An old-time term for a milk shake/cabinet/frappe/velvet made with chocolate syrup and vanilla ice cream is a **black and white**. Swap vanilla for chocolate in that recipe and you have an **all black**.

two lamps lit and no ship out. Extravagant and therefore wasteful. If there's no ship coming to shore, no need to waste whatever fuel is lighting those lamps.

wicked. Before "wicked" was the name of a Broadway musical, it was a way for many New Englanders to mangle the adverb "wickedly" by dropping the last syllable and making it a synonym for "very." An idea can be wicked good, a person can be wicked funny, a thing can be wicked pissa (cool). The *Cape Codder* newspaper even has an online feature called http://wickedlocalcapecod.com. To grammarians' ears this all sounds wicked awful, but colloquialisms seldom consult grammarians. "Wicked," as in the evil witch kind, harks back to the Old English *wicca*, or sorcerer. And who were among the oldest English to settle America? The Puritans of New England, of course, who were so concerned by wicked ways (consider Hester Prynne and *The Scarlet Letter*) that their descendants engaged in the shameful Salem witch trials. So it's only fitting that wicked should be part of the New England lexicon. (If nothing else, it makes for good folk etymology.) Even L.L. Bean has gotten into the act, with its Wicked Good Moccasins. That most un-Puritanical of writers, F. Scott Fitzgerald, gets a scarlet-lettered A for effort in trying to sound wicked good. In *This Side of Paradise*, one of his characters announces, "Phoebe and I are going to shake a wicked calf." Fitzgerald was, however, missing the customary second modifier—a wicked pretty calf, or a wicked sexy calf, perhaps. Blame it on his editor.

Jimmy Crack Corn? Try Johnny

The charming Rhode Island village of Usquepaugh is famous for two things: it's hard to get the spelling right, and it hosts a Harvest Festival celebrating the johnnycake. The **johnnycake** is no Johnny-come-lately to American cuisine. It's been around by that name since at least 1739 and is a sweeter iteration of a New England staple in the 1600s called **Indian cake**.

Essentially cornmeal with a little salt thrown in, it was also called a **no cake**. As in "No, thank you, I couldn't take another bite of salted cornmeal"? No. Actually, the name was a shortened version of *nokehick*, a Narragansett term meaning "soft." The Narragansetts were among the Native Americans in Rhode Island, and their cornmeal concoctions were soft.

The early colonists borrowed more than just words from their Native American neighbors: they also borrowed—and sometimes swiped—food sources. One of the most curious for these emigrating Europeans was this stuff called corn, an oddity in the Old World but a staple in the early days of the New. So essential did corn become that until shortly before the Revolutionary War, "meal" was all you had to say when referring to cornmeal.

The North and South diverged on what to call the

covering of the ear of corn. New Englanders called it the **husk**; Virginians referred to it as the **shuck**.

The no cake morphed into the **hoecake** in the mid-1700s and **ashcake** in the early 1800s. Both owe their names to the cooking method used: sometimes slapping the dough onto a flat hoe blade to cook, sometimes burying it in the ashes of a fire.

When "johnnycake" entered the lexicon in the mid-1700s, cooks had figured out that adding sugar to the (corn)meal sweetened the deal considerably. At least three theories as to the origin of the name get tossed around. It could be from the Native American *jonakin*, for cornmeal cakes, or from mispronouncing *Shawnee cake*. Or it could be "journey cake" with the *r* sound missing (as often happens in New England accents—the *r*'s show up where there are none, and disappear from where there are). Unlike bakery cakes, johnnycakes are flat and dense and thus may travel—or journey—well.

Occasionally in New England you might hear **bannock**. In Maine you might hear a distinction between **blackjacks**, gingerbread made with dark molasses, and **yellowjacks**, made with cornmeal.

It's not just New England where cornmeal is baked or fried (although Rhode Island takes its johnnycakes most seriously, with a Society for the Propagation of the Jonnycake Tradition, and cornmeal that's ground specifically for use in johnnycakes). Georgians mix cornbread and egg for **egg bread**. Virginians do the same, and they took to calling it **baddy bread**—as in "batter bread"—in the 1890s. In the Ozarks, that hard cornbread with no shortening is known as **barefoot bread**.

✳

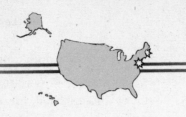

EAST JABIB

The Mid-Atlantic

Okay, who had the bright idea of putting Pittsburgh in the same chapter with New York and New Jersey, along with Philadelphia, Maryland, and Delaware? It's not diabolical, just geographical. And from a language perspective, it results in a delightful gallimaufry.

beef on weck. The signature roast beef sandwich of western New York State, which places like Schwabl's in Buffalo and Beef 'n' Barrel in Olean have been serving by the bucketloads for years. (Note to visitors wanting to fit in: there really is a difference between western and upstate New York.) Thin slices of roast beef are moistened au jus. But it's the weck that's the star of this show. "Weck" is short for "kummelweck," an amalgam of the German for "caraway" and "roll." This roll is topped with caraway seeds and kosher salt. Just pronounce it "wick"; everybody else does. And don't forget the horseradish.

belly-bumper. Sliding down the snowy hill on your sled, on your belly. Kids in Pennsylvania have been enjoying this bumpy ride since at least 1877, the first time the term appeared in print.

bridge-and-tunnel crowd. What transplants to Manhattan often call those who live over the bridges and through the tunnels in such far-off lands as Brooklyn, Queens, Long Island, and Jersey. The expression first appeared in, appropriately, the *New York Times*, in late 1977. It gained a little more traction in 1984, when Dan Jenkins used it in his book *Life Its Ownself*. But it remained a bit of a well-kept Manhattan secret (like Zabar's) until it migrated to movies. Kate Hudson, playing a Manhattanite in *Raising Helen*, spits it out like an epithet as she shudders at the possibility of being among the B&T crowd. There is, in fact, a Triborough Bridge and Tunnel Authority that services New York's boroughs (of which there are five, not three). A few other metropolitan areas have tried to adopt "bridge-and-tunnel" to refer to suburbanites who come to the city, among them San Francisco and Houston (Houston?). But their lingo just isn't the same; unless they're willing to stand ON LINE as New Yorkers do, they should give it up.

bubkes, as in "I got bubkes." You got squat, nada, nothing. Or at least, the smallest amount that it's possible to get. The word is Slavic and means "beans." (Think of the expression "it didn't amount to a hill of beans": it didn't amount to much.) This is a Yiddish expression frequently heard in New York—the city, not the state. But there are parts of New York State where, when it comes to state funding, the residents feel they get bubkes.

city chicken. A sort of bare-bones shish kebab, in that chunks of the stuff are impaled on skewers. Here's the kicker: city chicken is actually pork. It's been a well-known dish for many families in parts of Ohio, Pennsylvania, and New York State. One explanation for the name is that the skewered meat resembles a chicken leg. (In fact, in Milwaukee they call this **mock chicken leg**.) But there's also another theory. In the early part of the twentieth century, chicken was pricier than pork, so for those who couldn't afford the real thing, they could at least *call* it chicken. (Not to be outdone, the cowboys of the Old West called bacon **chuck-wagon chicken**.)

Croton cocktail. New York City tap water. The area gets its drinking water from the Croton Aqueduct, and it's good. Let's see if any New York restaurant decides to offer "free Croton cocktails" on its menus.

duck on davy. The name of a game that dates back to nineteenth-century Pennsylvania. Set a small rock (the duck) on top of a large rock (the davy). Then toss stones and try to knock the duck off the davy. Wonder how this would work as an app.

East Jabib. A metaphoric term for the back of beyond, aka Podunk, aka the middle of nowhere. You won't find any place called Jabib (or Japip), but you might find this expression used in the Philadelphia and New Jersey area. It's been a way to say boondocks, or to refer to a place that takes forever to get to, since the 1900s. If someone directs you to East Jabib, don't go. You can't program your GPS for Jabib. "Their house was so far out in the country, I felt like we were going to East Jabib and would never come back."

eat-'em-and-beat-'em. An old-time cafeteria-style restaurant that you used to find in New York City, but no more. Patrons would select their plates of food from a table, and then tally up their bill based on what they ate. Paying relied on an honor system—hence the cynical "beat 'em" in the name. In general, though, patrons came to eat and didn't try to beat the system.

egg cream. A soft drink made with neither egg nor cream, to which New Yorkers are apt to say, "And your point?" (They just don't think it matters.) It helps to be a New Yorker to understand what the big deal is about this blend of seltzer water, chocolate syrup, and milk. They've been slurping egg creams since the turn of the twentieth century, when an adventurous immigrant named Louis Auster first concocted the drink. Mixed just right, the ingredients froth into a creamy foam head, like well-beaten egg whites.

elevator apartment. An apartment building with an elevator. So who cares, you say. Probably nobody other than the people in New York City. Here, every little thing about real estate takes on big importance. The *New York Times* first used the expression "elevator apartment" in 1912, and it signaled more than merely the presence of an elevator. It meant you'd come up in the world because you didn't live in a fifth-floor walk-up.

floor-through. An apartment that takes up the entire floor. To all but Manhattan ears, "floor-through" sounds like a CATAWAMPUS way to say "through the floor." It's not. The phrase came on the Manhattan real estate scene in 1964. This was before prices of apartments there went through the roof—or roof-through, said the catawampus way.

Foggy Bottom. People in the Washington, DC, metro area say this with nary a snicker: Foggy Bottom is one of the oldest neighborhoods in the capital (hence the capital *F* and *B*). It's a 'hood that dates back to the late 1700s. Proximity to the Potomac makes it prone to river fog, and its early days as an industrial area made it susceptible to smog. But Foggy Bottom has since risen to the top in terms of desirable places to live: it's now registered as a U.S. historic district.

French flat. An apartment, or flat, inside what was once a private home. This is more New York City real estate talk and something you heard much more in the nineteenth century than now.

frizzled. The way some in Baltimore like their hot dogs: split and deep-fried. "Frizzled" is a portmanteau of "fry" and "sizzle." The word has been around since at least 1851, when Harriet Beecher Stowe used it in *Uncle Tom's Cabin*.

funeral pie. Raisin pie in Pennsylvania, so called because of its ubiquitous appearance at funerals since at least 1949.

grinnie. A chipmunk in western Pennsylvania.

gumband. A rubber band, if you're in Pittsburgh. German heritage is showing here. "Gum band" is just a couple of linguistic steps away from *Gummiring*, which is how the Germans say "rubber band." *Gummiband* is another version. (From gummibands to Gummi Bears?) The coal miners' rubber boots are also called **gum boots**. In Minnesota they kept the "rubber" but not the "band"—here a rubber band has been a **rubber binder** since at least the 1950s.

hang a Louie. Turn left, especially if you're in New York City, where you're most apt to be hanging these. Americans have been hanging varieties of lefts, rights, and U-ies since at least the 1960s. Why "Louie" is "left" is a bit of a mystery. One possibility is that "Louie" rhymes with "U-ie" and brings a certain poetry to these turns. Another is that Louis Lefkowitz, New York State's former attorney general, has a surname that sounds like "left" (he was New York City's unsuccessful candidate for mayor in 1961—perhaps because his politics were to the right). A third is that the boxer Joe Louis (1914–81) had a legendary left hook. In Boston, you'll occasionally hear the variation **bang a Louie**. Try driving in Boston and you'll get it. In Chicago, they're not so crazy about Louie, but they do like to **hang a Reggie** (right: it means right).

have a catch. In most other places in the country, kids and kids at heart say "let's play catch." But a number of New Yorkers don't *play*; they *have*. The expression might be a shortened way of saying "Let's have a game of catch." They've been having catches since the 1950s. Only the game of catch is had, though—other games, you play.

hon. What everyone calls everyone in Baltimore. You may want to go to the annual Honfest to get a taste of just how popular a greeting this is. It's the shortened version of "honey," of course. How sweet that a state known for its crabs has such a happy greeting.

jag-off. A jerk, an idiot, or as Pittsburgh natives might say, "one of the ultimate terms of derision when you were kids." To jag in Scots-Irish is to jab or prick, both annoying activities that someone who jags off—or goofs off—is likely to do, at least figuratively.

jug handles. The New Jersey way to make a left-hand turn by turning right: the lane goes to the right, then bends left across the road for a left turn. The term has nothing to do with love handles *or* jugs, so don't even go there. But when you go to New Jersey, you're apt to encounter jug handles on some of the roads you drive. Much like the cloverleaf, the name comes from the shape the turn takes. It's been around since the early 1960s. In Michigan, a comparable turn and twist is called the **Michigan left**.

Kennywood's open. "Your fly is open," if you happen to come unzipped in Pittsburgh. Kennywood is a local amusement park. There's really no good reason why people say Kennywood, except that it's a beloved mainstay of the area. In South Carolina, you could hear a comparable expression in the 1960s: **the hot dog stand is open**. In case you're wondering, Kennywood (the amusement park) is open most days in season from 10:30 a.m. to 10:00 p.m.

Kossuth cake. A rich sponge cake in which whipped cream usually plays a major part. In 1851 a Hungarian patriot named Louis Kossuth (can you see where this is going?) came to Baltimore on a one-man fund-raiser for the revolution. He would have done better had he gotten royalties on the cake that now bears his name. A local baker created it in Kossuth's honor.

Lucy Bowles. Try to avoid Lucy Bowles if you can, because it's "loose-y bowels" thinly disguised. People in parts of Pennsylvania, New Jersey, and New York State are among those apt to say "Lucy Bowles" for "diarrhea." This Lucy first appeared on the scene in 1965, just a couple years before that other memorable Lucy—the one in the Sky with Diamonds. If someone says, "Unfortunately, Lucy Bowles has decided to visit me today," you'd be smart to decide not to.

meet me between the lions. Which means we'll be meeting at a central spot on Fifth Avenue in Manhattan. Whoa—piranhas on Wall Street, yes. But lions on Fifth? Indeed. They are the stone sculptures that flank the main entrance to the New York Public Library on Forty-second Street and Fifth Avenue. New York's beloved mayor Fiorello La Guardia named the lions Patience and Fortitude. New Yorkers have long had such "meet me" expressions. At the beginning of the twentieth century, it was "meet me at the Hyphen," the affectionate slang for the newly merged Waldorf and Astoria hotels. Then F. Scott Fitzgerald popularized "meet me under the clock" at the Biltmore Hotel. Hard to do these days, since the Biltmore is no more. But Patience and Fortitude still reign, the undisputed literary lions of New York.

moving night or **move night.** The night before Halloween, when the mischievous in Maryland go around the neighborhoods moving things—porch furniture off one porch and onto another, for example. It's kind of a warm-up to the Big Boo on the thirty-first.

mung you. Amongst you, but really another way that people in Delaware and Maryland say "you-all." "Mung you" has been amongst our recorded regionalisms since 1938. "Mung you coming to dinner? If so, I'll set places for three more."

neb-nose. A nosy person if you're from Pittsburgh. Saying neb-nose is a bit like saying nosy nosy, as "neb" is, in fact, another word for nose—or beak or snout. You still hear some Brits saying neb, as Ringo Starr did (fittingly, given his own considerable one). So being nebby is the same as being nosy. "Don't be a neb-nose" can be a somewhat more tactful way to say "mind your own business."

nosh. Have a little something to eat, a snack, a taste. This delightful Yiddish expression is heard in many a New York delicatessen. The German word for "to nibble" is *naschen*. "Nosh on this" is how you might hear someone schooled in Yiddish invite you to have a bite, especially if they've offered to **make you a plate**.

on line. In line. No, says the New Yawker: it's *on* line. New Yorkers (from the city, not the state) are the only people who don't stand *in* line; they stand *on* it—perhaps because of their famous impatience with just standing around. You'll also hear the expression in parts of South Florida, which is sometimes called the

Sixth Borough of Manhattan because so many expatriate New Yorkers move there. (British visitors to the Big Apple, who stand in/on line better than anyone, are puzzled: for them it's a matter of getting "in the queue.") The *New York Times* does its Gray Lady best to discourage the term in its paper, reminding reporters in its famed stylebook that the rest of the country stands *in* line. Ironically, at least once in its history, the *Times* has been caught out standing on line in a story. But that was back in 1975, and on April first—so perhaps the reporter was just fooling. "If you want to get half-price tickets to that Broadway show, you'll have to stand on line."

pencil point. Skinny pasta. Trenton is known for it. The tubes are about as big around as a—you guessed it—pencil. The ends are cut on the diagonal—there's your point. A fancier name is penne, but where's the fun in that?

piss-a-bed. A dandelion. A *dandelion*? Yep, that's what it's called in the old folk tale from the 1830s, which all but guaranteed that any kids who picked dandelions would pee in their beds.

plotz. To burst or explode, figuratively speaking. New Yorkers reach for this Yiddish word both when they're annoyed and when they're not. They could be so aggravated, they could plotz. Or be laughing so hard, they might plotz. This multipurpose word is rooted in the German *platzen*, "to burst."

pungey. An old Delmarva name (Delaware-Maryland-Virginia) for an oyster boat.

redd up. Straighten up or tidy up, Pennsylvania style (especially Pittsburgh). Actually, in the 1800s and even through the mid-1900s, people said "redd up" in more parts of the country. You'd hear the term in Illinois, Kansas, Arkansas, Ohio, and West Virginia, but it remains in use only in parts of Pennsylvania. "Redd" suggests "ready," but the word itself goes way back to a sixteenth-century legal term, "void and redd," meaning vacated for the next person.

schlep. The New Yorker way to lug packages. This Yiddishism has its roots in the German *schleppen*, "to drag." But why schlep when you can have all those bags delivered?

what a schmo. The way a jerk is often identified in the metropolitan New York area. Combine Yiddish and English and you have what Leo Rosten (*The Joys of Yiddish*) calls Yinglish, which is what "schmo" is.

Scuffletown. A rough town, where you can get into a scuffle if you're not careful. The *Baltimore Sun* christened the word in print in 1941.

table money. Household money—the part of your cashed paycheck that you put on the table for food, rent, and other necessities. Jimmy Breslin titled his 1990 novel *Table Money*.

That Big Honkin' Hunk of Sandwich

If you're from the Philly area, you know this sandwich to be the **hoagie**. Other parts of the country call it a **bomber**, **sub** (as in "submarine," whose shape it resembles), **wedge**, or **hero**, the latter being the American way to almost say the Greek *gyro*.

New Englanders call it the **grinder**, although some Bostonians refer to it as a **spuckie**. That term is a faint nod to an Italian word for the roll the innards sit in. Certain New Jerseyites know it as the **zep** (think of the shape of a zeppelin—like a **torpedo**, which is another name some folks use). Old-timers might call it the **Dagwood** or **Bumstead**, named after the *Blondie* comic strip character who's always building a huge stack of cold cuts between two big pieces of bread.

New Orleanians use rich French bread and call the meal a **po'boy**. The early version of these "poorboys," as tourists of the nineteenth century called them, was intended for people of impecunious means. It cost ten cents in 1921. A comparable New Orleans concoction is the **muffuletta**—or "muf-a-lotta," as the joke goes. The name comes from the Sicilian for the kind of bread that's used. Even in French-drenched New Orleans, the hoagie road leads to **Italian**—which is what this sandwich is called in Maine and parts of the Midwest.

And that brings us back to "hoagie." Philadelphia claims the crown for this coinage. The term may have come from "hog." True enough, you can pig out with one of these bulky bonanzas, but this hog may have come from a wartime shipyard in Philly called Hog Island where many Italian Americans worked and where they fortified themselves with these hefty sandwiches.

The hoagie story beats this one for "grinder," which *The Saturday Evening Post* put forth in 1955: you call it a grinder because you grind your teeth when chowing down. That ranks right down there on the ho-hum scale with why a cabinet (see page 19) is so called.

two cents plain. A glass of soda water. You heard this in the New York City area back in the 1950s. It was a time when soft drinks were mixed at a soda fountain using flavorings, or syrups, and plain soda water. When you wanted just the soda water and not the syrup, you asked for two cents plain.

White Plates. A derogatory term for New Yorkers that refers to the current New York State license plate, which is mainly white. "White Plates" is how New Jerseyites exact verbal revenge on New Yorkers. New Jerseyites would explain it this way: "White Plates are what we call New Yorkers who have decided to live in New Jersey for the open space, and then clear-cut all the trees on their property."

yinz, or yunz. "You" in the plural, in Pittsburghese. Since regular English doesn't know enough to differentiate between one of you and five of yous, at least some of us do. "Y'all" is the common Southern expression; "youz guys" is the clunky stand-in. But people from Pittsburgh ("Pixburg," as some natives call it) say something closer to the "yez" that can still be heard in some Irish voices and that's been around since at least the 1800s.

The Oys of Yiddish

"Yiddish," wrote Leo Rosten in the preface to his classic *The Joys of Yiddish*, "is the Robin Hood of languages. It steals from the linguistically rich to give to the fledgling poor. It shows not the slightest hesitation in taking in houseguests."

No wonder many Americans today steal from it (even if unwittingly), reach for it, or are in some way delighted by it: Yiddish has a knack comparable to English for rising to the linguistic occasion. Why settle for the rather flat-sounding "congratulations" when you can utter the more exuberant and punchy **mazel tov**?

Yiddish is not Hebrew but it is, of course, a way of speaking for many of the Jewish faith. It's also a parlance and a nuance that has come to form some of the linguistic contours of New York City. What—you think New York would sound the way it does—and the way only New York can sound—without the influence of Yiddish? As if.

Yiddish actually got its start around the tenth century, a language that evolved among Jews living in Germany and, later, the countries of eastern Europe. It's been spoken longer than it's been written; the first Yiddish known to be transcribed was in a thirteenth-century prayer book.

Isaac Bashevis Singer, the Nobel Prize–winning

writer beloved as a Yiddish storyteller, described Yiddish as a language that "muddles through." A language, in other words, that's just like most of us. What's not to love?

So there's no arrogance in Yiddish, but there's plenty of arrogance in the Yiddish word **chutzpah** (or "chutzpa," or even "hutzpa"). Saying that someone has chutzpah is a way to say that person is audacious or has, um, guts. There's often a tinge of admiration that goes along with chutzpah, for the sheer gall of it all.

It takes chutzpah to offer a **schmear**—not in the sense of a dollop of cream cheese, although the word is also used in this way, but in the sense of a bribe. Not that anybody in New York ever expects to be schmeared, of course. As if.

Such an individual would be a **no-goodnik**, which is considered a Yinglish word (Yiddish + English). The Slavic nik is a popular appendage to other terms as well. Think of "beatnik," for one. When the Russians launched Sputnik in 1957, they also launched "nik" as a way to cobble together various colorful expressions.

Colorful they like, but don't expect unsentimental New Yorkers to fall for any **schmaltz**, or gushy emotional stuff. This Yiddishism for corny has the more literal meaning of chicken fat.

Someone who's a flunky or a hanger-on is a

nokhshleper. Notice how neatly SCHLEP (or "shlep"), meaning "drag," fits into this word. Nokhshlepers can be a drag to have around, as they're forever tagging along and often dragging you down. It's enough to drive someone crazy, or **meshuga**.

Next time somebody really screws up and commits the faux pas from hell, brush it off with a mention of **bulbe**. That's the Yiddish way to say gaffe, and it literally means potato. In the theater, a **bulbenik** is one who flubs his or her lines. (Should there be a new coinage of "spuddering" for when these potato-heads start stammering and stuttering?)

Tchotchke is a dismissive word for mere toys or trifles. Lots of retailers sell such trinkets. They take on many forms, but their common denominator is that of dust collector. "Tchotchke" usually refers to objects but is sometimes used to describe people who fit into this category as well.

To **kvetch** is to complain (komplain?). A kvetch is one who complains. A lot. All the time. Incessantly. Chronically. Whine whine whine. Will you stop with this kvetching?! The Yiddish *kvetshn* draws from the German *quetschen*, meaning "to squeeze or crush." Sort of like the way you want to strangle a kvetch who won't stop kvetching.

Kvell rhymes with "swell," and it means to swell or beam with pride. Parents kvell over their children's accomplishments, for example. The word harks back to the German *quellen*, meaning "to gush or swell." Usually you kvell over something positive that makes you proud and happy. But sometimes you kvell over another person's bad luck. What—you've never gloated over someone else's misfortune? As if.

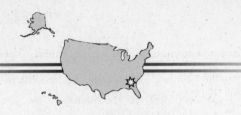

BLESS YOUR HEART

The South

It covers a big area, and you're not always likely to hear the same expression in every state. Certainly the dialects differ from one part to another. But chances are one Southerner will understand another. The rest of us can gape and be grateful for the imagination and humor they inject into the language.

One caveat: South Florida is only a tiny bit Southern, despite its latitude. Great influxes of people from the New York City and Chicago areas infuse it with Northeastern and Midwestern sensibilities, while a significant Latino population (often called Hispanic here) adds a strong Latin flavor. South Florida is where you sit overlooking the Intracoastal Waterway (the closest thing to a Midwestern river) as you munch on lox and bagel and chase it with a café Cubano.

absolute auction. In Kentucky, they've been auctioning land like this since at least 1876, when the term was first recorded here. Absolute auction means the property is absolutely, positively sold to the highest bid, regardless of what the dollar amount is. Today you'll find absolute auctions throughout the country.

Adam's off-ox, as in **"don't know him from Adam's off-ox."** In other words, you don't know him from Adam. The "off-ox" simply underscores how much you don't know him. Former president Bill Clinton, an Arkansas native, bethumped the media and many Americans when he reached for this 1894 expression during a 1993 press conference. Next time you're driving a team of oxen, notice how you can barely see the one on the other side from where you're walking. That's the off-ox. The expression is sometimes garbled into amusing mondegreens of "Adam's all-fox" and "Madam's off-ox."

Arkansas toothpick. A big knife with a long bad blade. They started using the term in Tennessee back in the 1830s. The implication is that the person wielding such a toothpick also wields an unfair advantage in a fight.

beat the hound out of the big dog. In the Carolinas, when you cut someone of self-importance down to size, this is how you say it. Folks here have been saying it since at least 1847. It's all the sweeter if the self-important one was so puffed up as to be a **big dog with a brass collar**, another expression almost as old. "The governor's had to apologize—don't that beat the hound out of the big dog."

bless your heart. Sometimes heard as **bless your little bones**, this is a term of endearment—most of the time (read on). As rooted in the speech of the South as the phrase may be, it also pops up in, of all places, Dickens. "Why, bless your heart alive," exclaims Mrs. Cratchit in *A Christmas Carol*. And she sure wasn't talking to Scrooge. But that brings up the flip side of this blessing. It's also a phrase that polite Southerners reach for when they really want to curse you rather than bless you. When this is the case, the more emphasis on *heart*, the more quietly they're seething. This use of "bless" calls to mind another Southernism, **blessing out**. It means the opposite of what it sounds like: you're not being blessed, you're being scolded. People have been getting blessed out in the South since at least Civil War days.

blowed. The way something becomes hugely successful, if it's an Oklahoman talking. People who are amazed at how this happened are apt to say, "Well, I'm blowed." Nebraskans were using the term at the turn of the twentieth century to mean "I'll be darned." It sounds so American grown, but we're blowed if it doesn't appear in a comparable context in that most English of places, yet another Charles Dickens novel. "One blowed thing and another," one of the characters in *A Tale of Two Cities* pronounces.

boomalally. A soldier marching in step to the music. A woman in South Carolina is credited with coming up with the term in the 1950s. She was inspired by the drums of marching band music, which go *boom*.

boweevil. The Oklahoma way to say "boll weevil" and, by extension, worthless. Cotton pickers know boll weevils to be the beetles that prey on their crop: a real pest. In the 1930s, some Californians started calling novice workers in the oil fields boll weevils, a term that Oklahomans were using by 1941 (and Texans soon after). Anytime you're named after a bug, it's not good. A boweevil, being an inexperienced worker, is considered a no-account.

cat 1, cat 3, etc. Category 1, Category 3, etc. Part of the new disaster-speak evolving in South Florida and other places where hurricanes hit, ever since hurricanes started hitting with more frequency a few years ago. The category number denotes how high the winds are and therefore how destructive the storm. The higher the number, the worse the winds. You always hope for a cat 1 and fear for your life in a cat 5. Florida also has a state Cat Fund, "cat" in this case being short for "catastrophe," the frequent outcome of a cat 2 or worse hurricane.

catawampus. Askew, crooked, awry. "Catty-wampus" or "kitty-wampus" is how you'll often hear it—much like "cater-cornered" becomes "kitty-corner." The Scots word for twist is *wampish*, and that may well be where this kitty gets its wampus. But the word is considered American, not English. It's one of our very own colloquial coinages from the mid-1800s, and it sounds like the discombobulation it suggests.

chughole. Somewhere between a sinkhole and a mudhole. You're likely to find a pothole by this name in Kentucky especially, and possibly Arkansas and Oklahoma, too. Back in 1948, a Louisville newspaper told its readers the "chug" came from "ug," the pronouncement a wagon driver would make when he hit one of these holes. We wouldn't be surprised if the driver uttered a lot more than "ug." Another, more plausible explanation is that "chughole" is a variation of "chuck hole," this use of "chuck" meaning to throw or toss. You very possibly could get thrown or tossed when you hit a chughole. This takes us back to the French *choquer*, to shock or shake up.

come-here. In parts of Virginia, a come-here is not from here. A come-here comes from somewhere else (**from away**, a Cape Codder or Bonacker might say). A come-here might live here forever more, but he or she still came from elsewhere. Only the natives came here long enough ago not to be come-heres.

we've come to the goat's house for wool. Where we are is not where we want to be, because what we're looking for, they don't have. There are two ways to approach the origin of this statement. The first is that goats don't have wool, sheep do, so obviously we're in the wrong place. The second is to overlay the expression with what some northeast Texans have been known to call a goat house, as recorded back in 1970: an outhouse.

come up. In North Carolina and other parts of the South, particularly among African Americans, you don't *grow* up in a place, you *come* up. Southerners have been coming up since at least 1953, when the expression was first recorded.

Conch Republic. In these United States there are fifty states, the protectorate of Puerto Rico, the District of Columbia . . . and the republic of Key West, better known as the Conch Republic. It was a New York newspaper in the 1850s that pointed out the prevalence of Bahamians in Key West. Darned if these "conch men" weren't pros at diving for conch, the local shellfish with the graceful, pink-tinged shell. ("Conch" comes from the Greek word for shellfish.) Key Westers long ago figured out that they live on their own special planet and thus declared themselves the Conch Republic. They seceded on April 23, 1982, but apparently nobody in Washington got the memo.

crooked as a dog's hind leg. A deceitful, dishonest cur. Watch how easily and deeply dogs can scrunch up their back legs. You can't get much crookeder than that. Crooked is okay if you're a dog, but not if you're a human. It's the kind of expression a Virginia gentleman summons when the strongest of epithets is called for.

dirt-dog poor. Extremely poor. Southerners add the "dog" to emphasize just how dirt-poor someone is. Why "dirt"? Because you're so poor, you have only an earthen floor.

fairs up, as in "as soon as it fairs up a mite." When the weather improves somewhat, it fairs up a mite—in other words, it clears up. Some version of this has been summoned to describe better weather since at least 1836, from "faired away" to "fair off."

F.F.V. First Families of Virginia. The acronym was first put to paper in 1847 and signals that you're speaking about one of the long-established, prominent families of Old Dominion.

fine as frog's hair. First off, have you ever actually *seen* frog's hair? Thus "fine as frog's hair" can describe something small, as it did when the expression was heard in Kansas in 1897. Or it can describe the smallest detail. But this is too fine an expression to leave to just one or two meanings, so by at least 1905 someone in Arkansas was using it to indicate a sense of well-being, as in mighty fine. To make your point even more strongly, you might say "fine as frog's hair split in the middle." You wouldn't think that something you can't even see could render a statement of such utility and versatility. But never underestimate the Southern talent for putting a fine point on a phrase. By 1916 people were saying "fine as frog's hair" in Indiana and Kentucky, and it appeared in a cartoon in San Francisco. Leapfrog to the 1950s, and the phrase assumed its third meaning, of something that doesn't exist—like **dog's eggs**.

fixing. How Southerners plan: they're fixing to do something. In the West, home of Annie Oakley and other sure shots, they're *aiming* to do it. In the North, they're *going* to do it. But in the South, they're actually echoing some of the earliest English spoken in America—albeit in Massachusetts. "I got up to fix to go to Boston," reads an entry in a 1794 Massachusetts diary. Even earlier, in 1716, a Massachusetts writer observed that the ship captain "fixes for another Expedition." The word comes from the Latin verb for fasten, which suggests how strongly you latch onto whatever you're fixing to do. A corollary use is when someone says, "**I had my mouth fixed** for a piece of that cake." This "fix" is next-door neighbor to "fixate."

frog strangler. Frogs again—this time as a metaphor for a heavy rain, first recorded in the 1950s. You can also describe it as a **frog-choker** or **frog drownder**. (In some parts of the South, and as far west as Illinois, it's a **goose-drownder**. In parts of Florida, it's a **palmetto pounder**.) By Southern GULLY WASHER standards, raining mere cats and dogs is for wusses.

gallinipper. A mosquito. But call it a gallinipper and you create quite a buzz. It makes it, quite possibly, the Loch Ness monster of biting bugs. "Gallinipper" is the stuff of folk etymology. Among its multitudinous variations is **granny-nipper**. And while you're most likely to hear the phrase in southern sections of the country, folks in New England were writing about "Gurninippers" back in the 1600s. Its "biting causeth an itching . . . which provoketh scratching," they saideth. Early definitions of the mosquito distinguished between your average-Joe stinger and your major stinger, the gallinipper. Being bitten by the latter was, according to an 1831 newspaper account, like being "pricked by a stiletto." These bugs sucked a gallon of blood, maintained an early-nineteenth-century account. No nip-and-tuck with these 'nippers—more like nip-and-suck.

givey. Muggy. When it's humid, it's givey: the earth is damp enough to give, and it makes tobacco leaves do the same. That was how Southerners originally used the term back in the 1850s, as they surveyed their important crop. Try saying "It's a givey day today" the next time the humidity is off the charts.

gnat's-bristle clean. Clean as a whistle isn't clean enough for some folks in these parts—they want it as clean as the bristle on a gnat. Now, don't go getting hung up on whether gnats have bristles and if they're clean. You'll drain this colorful expression of all its Kodachrome. Nattering about gnats has been going on in South Carolina since at least 1840. The expression also signifies something very small, particularly when suggesting precision. If it **fits to a gnat's heel**, it fits like a glove. Other parts of gnat a*gnat*omy are also sometimes pressed into service. **Fine as a gnat's whiskers** was recorded in Kentucky in 1960; **sharp enough to split the hair on a gnat's ass** was proclaimed in Tennessee a few years before that. The insect's eyebrow, eyelash, and toenail also occasionally get in on the act.

go 'round your elbow to get to your thumb. Go out of your way to get where you're going. Southerners often follow such a circuitous route in conversation. Thank goodness the GPS is a new phenomenon, or we might not have this colorful expression, which was making the rounds by 1914 at least. The inverse route—around your thumb to get to your elbow—takes you just as far out to there when all you wanted to do was get to here. But there are worse things you can do with your elbows. In Alaska, there's an ancient native game dubbed the **elbow walk**, where only your elbows and toes can touch the ground.

gully washer. A real soaker of a rainstorm. It's pelting so hard that the ditches (gullies) are spewing forth water.

ice house. A local establishment that sells ice but, even more important, serves beer. Patrons started frequenting ice houses in the 1920s, when local businesses started storing and selling ice.

ill. No, you're not ailing. You're either bad tempered or naughty. It could be, and used to be, worse. In the 1850s, this "ill" meant vicious.

jackleg. Someone who's incompetent and, to add insult to injury, often dishonest to boot. Mark Twain described Jim this way in *Tom Sawyer Abroad*: "Jim was a kind of jack legged tailor." You heard the word a lot in the mid-1800s, often to describe lawyers, doctors, and preachers. "Jack" has long been a polite epithet. "Any common fellow" was Jack, as early as the fourteenth century.

Kentucky colonel. An honorary designation bestowed on those deemed to be honorable. Guess what state this term originated in? (And then we'll move on to Grant's Tomb.) So you go into your local KFC and you see the iconic mug shot of the white-haired bearded gentleman they call Colonel Sanders and you wonder, is this guy for real as far as the colonel business? Well, yes, but in a Kentucky-colonel kind of way. After the War of 1812, the governor of Kentucky rewarded one of the outstanding officers in his state's militia with the military rank of colonel. The idea stuck. By the late 1800s, it had become an honorary designation that the governor bestowed on an admirable person of merit. In 1935 the governor conferred the title on Harland Sanders, to be forever thereafter known as the Colonel Sanders of Kentucky Fried Chicken. Those who receive the distinction can join the Honorable Order of Kentucky Colonels, a charitable organization that does good deeds. And no, not all Kentucky colonels are from Kentucky—Johnny Depp for one, Tiger Woods for another.

knee baby. The child who can (barely) stand, and who comes up to just about your knee. An African American expression long associated with North Carolina, "knee baby" also suggests that there's another, younger baby in the picture—one not yet old enough to reach your knee.

low-bush lightning. Illegal liquor—what many call moonshine. The rural parts of Florida are where you're likely to hear the expression, and this is a state that's on a first-name basis with lightning. The term was popular during Prohibition, which today might be called the era of DIY whiskey.

mash the lights. Turn off the lights. But you mash them only in the southern part of the country. It's "mash" in the sense of "press" or "press on." Which is perhaps why some of us press our clothes, rather than iron them—we could actually be mashing them, as was heard in Texas back in the 1890s.

mean as a suck-egg dog. Mean in the extreme, and Southerners mean this literally. They can't abide the unconscionable act of a dog breaking into a chicken coop and scarfing down all the eggs. "Suck-egg dogs," when used to describe humans, means they are no-account good-for-nothings.

mulligrubs. The blues, mainly in the South. Noah Webster featured the word in his 1806 *Compendious Dictionary of the English Language*, defining it as "a twisting of the guts, sullenness." The word comes from "mulliegrums," which in turn comes from "megrim," which goes all the way back to the Middle English word for migraine. Life was full of headaches even then.

nice to see you. A greeting that some Southerners, especially Georgians, extend even if they've never laid eyes on you before. Sure, you could say "nice to meet you," but what if you had, in fact, already met the person but forgotten you did? "Nice to see you" spares you both that embarrassment. You can text it, too: N2CU.

not enough sense to bell a buzzard. This is akin to not having enough sense to come in out of the rain. The phrase got on the linguists' radar in the 1960s. To bell means to attach a bell to a buzzard. Say what? It sure seems that someone who doesn't have enough sense to do such a fool thing might just be pretty smart, after all.

Oklahoma rain. It's been raining like this in Oklahoma since at least 1919. It's the same as an **Idaho rainstorm** (1934) and an **Arizona cloudburst** (1966). They're all ways to refer to sandstorms or dust storms. What—you were expecting a gully-washing FROG STRANGLER? So if you say "It's as dry as an Oklahoma rain," you're suggesting near-desert conditions.

Old Scratch. The devil. Although you hear this more in the South, the term originated in New England, in the early 1800s. In Stephen Vincent Benét's short story of 1937, "The Devil and Daniel Webster," that devil is called Old Scratch. Even earlier was Washington Irving's "Devil and Tom Walker." Old Englanders have been using the term since the 1740s. Old Norse probably gave us Old Scratch, as *skratte* meant "devil" in that language. Today some lottery tickets are called scratch tickets, and while there's no etymological bloodline between this scratch and Old Scratch, some would say that gambling is the work of the devil.

poor as Job's turkey. Very poor indeed. In the Old Testament, God tested Job's faith by divesting him of all his worldly goods. So far, so good. But a *turkey* in the Old Testament? No, Job didn't have turkeys, but Americans did, including Virginians, among whom this phrase was recorded back in the 1820s. For a while New Englanders used the expression, too. A Massachusetts sailor divested of his clothes by the captain of a ship reported in 1838 that he was left "in the situation of Job's turkey, without a feather to fly with."

short-pot. To shortchange someone, and deliberately so. Oklahomans aren't the only ones to short-pot, but they are the ones who are known for saying it.

Siscoed. The way some in Oklahoma will cry foul. It dates back to a college football game in 1947 between the Texas Longhorns and the Oklahoma SOONERS. The ref, Jack Sisco, made a call that worked against the Sooners, and they lost. "We got Siscoed" is another way to say "we were robbed."

Sooners. These were the Oklahoma settlers who showed up sooner than everyone else during the Oklahoma land run of the late 1800s. A few years later, in 1908, the University of Oklahoma christened its football team Sooners.

stay safe. A roundabout way of saying "don't get blown away." In this sense the expression is relatively new, having developed within the past eight years or so. Its growth tracks with the increased number of hurricanes hitting the United States. "Stay safe" is an expression you'll hear in places like South Florida when a hurricane warning is in effect. It's a way of acknowledging the ill wind that blows no good without having to mention it directly.

Northern and Southern

Just as Brits call the front of the car the bonnet and Yanks call it the hood, Northerners and Southerners have different words for the same things. Only generally speaking, of course, as Americans' inveterate hankering to roam and take their words with them means there are always exceptions. But here are a few words to help you pass as what you're not. (You're on your own as far as nailing the accent.)

North	South
bag	sack
carry	tote
pail	bucket
throw	chuck
frying pan	skillet
faucet	spigot
frosting	icing
power	current
guess	reckon
muggy	close

Sunday pipe, as in "down the Sunday pipe." You swallowed something the wrong way and now you're choking because it went down the wrong pipe—that is, the Sunday pipe. This is true even if you choke on a Sunday. The day suggests something special (think "Sunday best"), which is not too far off from indicating something out of the ordinary. Try not to be wearing your Sunday best when something goes down the Sunday pipe.

swamp cabbage. Heart of palm. Which name do you think goes over better on the menu of a fancy restaurant? "Swamp cabbage" is a Southernism, since the place has a fair number of swamps as well as palms. Cut out the hearts of the palms, boil them as you would cabbage, and you have what's become a delicacy. And it doesn't taste anything like cabbage. The palm of choice is the sabal, the official palm of Florida.

we're waiting on you. We're waiting for you, in non-Southern. Northerners may mistake "waiting on you" as another form of that famous Southern hospitality, but don't expect to *be* waited on when someone in the South *is* waiting on you. They're just waiting *for* you. *Waiting on Godot*, anyone?

Tea: How Sweet It Is

Nobody talked about the Boston Tea Party of December 16, 1773, until more than fifty years later. Naturally, Americans knew about the revolt before then, but they just didn't give it a name till long after it happened. Had the British not imposed their threepence-a-pound tax on tea on the colonies, Americans might well be more of a nation of tea drinkers than we are. Instead, patriots drank a concoction called liberty tea, a stirring euphemism for hot water with some local flowers tossed in. Thank goodness we won the Revolution.

Even so, the Brits still controlled the tea trade during the 1800s, thanks in large part to first Joseph Tetley and then Sir Thomas Lipton. American ingenuity finally prevailed during the middle of that century, when two merchants figured out a way to buy tea directly from the ships, making it far cheaper in the shops. Thus was born the A&P. Although those who remember it probably think of it as a supermarket, the A&P started as the Great Atlantic and Pacific Tea Company.

And so Americans went back to having tea parties again, this time not throwing the stuff away. In the 1870s these parties were sometimes called kettle-drums, after the name of the percussion instruments that once doubled as fashionable tea tables. Much of the tea Americans drank through the nineteenth century was green tea. "Iced tea" entered the lexicon in the 1860s. By this time enterprising Americans, particularly in the South, had already figured out that you could lace cold tea with liquor and call it a **punch**.

At the sizzling hot Saint Louis World's Fair in 1904, iced tea entered the pantheon of great American summertime drinks. Prohibition helped to popularize it further, as it provided an alternative to alcohol. Uh-huh. (Just remember that Long Island iced tea doesn't have a drop of tea in it but does have plenty of booze.)

Today, it's not so much about the ice as it is the sugar. Sweet iced tea, or simply **sweet tea**, is the anthem of the South. In fact, you are likely to see "tea" and "unsweet tea" on a Southern menu. There's no indication of hot or iced, which is why it's good to specify hot tea if that's what you want. It's naturally assumed that, given the heat that drapes the South so much of the year, who would want their tea hot? Southerners ordering their tea north of the Mason-Dixon not only have to make sure it's iced but that it's sweet as well.

But there's sweet, and then there's Southern, sweet-tea sweet. The secret is to add the sugar (or simple syrup) *before* the tea is iced, while it's still warm and brewing. In fact, a Georgia state representative toyed with proposing such a bill as state law. It was a joke, he said. Uh-huh.

And don't be afraid to bring it on in the sugar

department. Sweet tea often has more sugar than soft drinks. Not for nothin' are Southerners famous for saying "sugar."

The **"house wine of the South"** is how Dolly Parton's character in the film *Steel Magnolias* described sweet tea. Fittingly, it was South Carolina that first grew tea in the United States; it is now the state's "official hospitality beverage." Some of those tea leaves are finding their way into a brand of the new **sweet tea vodka**, which satisfies two cravings at once. Throw in some lemonade and you've got yourself a **John Daly.**

Prefer an **Arnold Palmer**? That's also known as a **half and half**: half iced tea and half lemonade. Still sweet, but not sweet enough to be Southern.

the weary dismals. Tennessee is where you're most likely to hear this melodious way to say depressed or in a funk. "Weather to give a man the weary dismals," grouses a character the author William Least Heat-Moon meets up with in Tennessee in his *Blue Highways*. "Dismal" as a noun goes back as early as Revolutionary days and the letters of John and Abigail Adams: "the spleen, the vapors, the dismals." The word can trace its ancestry back to the Latin *diēs malī*, which roughly translates to "bad hair day" (okay, just "bad day"). Swamps in the South are sometimes called dismals, like the Great

Dismal Swamp National Wildlife Refuge that Virginia and North Carolina share.

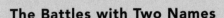

The Battles with Two Names

Some Americans called it the Civil War and others called it the War Between the States. The soldiers who fought the battles often knew them by different names. Union armies were inclined to name battles after the nearby terrain—a body of water, or a mountain or hill. Confederate armies were apt to name them after a well-known structure, or the town or village nearby. Here are some of the battles with two names.

Confederate Name	Union Name
Leesburg (town)	Ball's Bluff (bluff)
Manassas (railroad junction)	Bull Run (stream)
Murfreesboro (town)	Stones River (river)
Sharpsburg (town)	Antietam (creek)

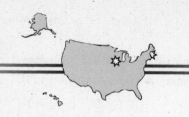

I'LL COME WITH

The Midwest

Location and vocation play major roles in the kinds of expressions you're likely to hear in America's middle. It is in the Midwest that we come to appreciate the differences between city and country living. Chicagoans may be intimately familiar with sliders, but don't ask most of them what it means to cook for the threshers on a Minnesota farm.

brat. This brat is not the obnoxious little kid; it's sausage-shorthand for bratwurst. And it's practically the state food of Wisconsin. Say "ahhh" and you'll say the *a* right. *Brat* means "roast or bake" in German; *wurst* means "sausage"; and there you have what many Wisconsinites would rather have than a hot dog. And don't even think of sticking your brat in a hot dog bun.

If it goes in anything (other than your mouth), it should be a **Sheboygan**, a hard roll that's also the name of a Wisconsin town. A TV station in Madison has been known to do a promotion called "Take your brat to work today." With pleasure, say brat lovers.

bubbler. A water fountain in parts of Illinois and Wisconsin. Not the big water dispensers you find in offices and even the kitchens of some homes, but the water fountains you find outdoors and in airports, where the water bubbles up from the spigot. If you're in Rhode Island or a few other parts of New England, you're probably saying, "Hold on there. Bubbler ["bub-luh"] is what *we* say." We hate to burst your bubbler, but folks in parts of the Midwest have been heard to say this since at least 1911.

cheese curds freshly squeaked. Newborn cheese, in a manner of speaking. Any Wisconsinite worth his or her whey will tell you that freshly squeaked is when cheese curds are best. Curd is cheese, usually cheddar, before it's processed and aged—sort of like just-born. The squeak is literal: these soft little nuggets squeal when you chew them. You get the best squeak when the curds are not yet a day old. Some bars serve cheese curds as if they were peanuts.

cooking for the threshers. Feeding the multitudes—or at least, a large gathering. In Minnesota farm communities, it used to be that the one threshing machine in the community would be pulled from farm to farm to help harvest the grain. Everybody would pitch in for this **threshing run** to help with each other's harvest. When it was your turn to use the thresher, you had to feed everybody who was helping. This might be as many as thirty people ("Hon, there's a few more for lunch today . . ."). And it might go on for four days.

Cream City. A nickname for Milwaukee that dates back to the mid-1800s. In a place so well-known for beer that it's also called **Brew City**, the "cream" must refer to the foam that bubbles up in a glass of beer, right? Nope. Cream is the color of the bricks that came from the area in the nineteenth century. They even became known as Cream City bricks. These days Milwaukee has another nickname, **Ill Mill**, usually said with more affection than ill will.

davenport. A sofa or a couch. You would think that, since the term is most often heard in the Midwest, it's somehow connected to Davenport, Iowa. It's not. In the 1880s, the A. H. Davenport Company was a leading maker of sofas. Like "thermos" and "escalator," its name became a generic term, with "davenport" meaning sofa. But the company was miles away from Iowa; it was in Boston.

feeling donsie. Not a good way to feel, because it means you're not feeling good. People have been feeling donsie, or dauncy, for a long time. It's an eighteenth-century word from the Scottish Gaelic *donas*, which means "ill."

doodinkus. Thingamajig, whatchamacallit, doohickey in Nebraska.

Double Domer. Someone with two degrees from the University of Notre Dame in Indiana. (The really overachieved are the Triple Domers.) The name comes from the iconic Golden Dome on the campus's Main Building. They don't dumb down at Notre Dame—they dome up.

feest. Filthy. You're likely to hear someone of Dutch ancestry say this, as the word comes from the Dutch word meaning to loathe or be disgusted with. It's had a parallel meaning of unclean or untidy since the turn of the twentieth century. If someone says to you, "Your house is absolutely feest," hand them the mop and tell them to start cleaning.

I'll have a four-way. Or a three-way, or a five-way. You hear this a lot in Cincinnati. Don't think people who say it are kinky—they're just hungry for some of Cincinnati's Skyline Chili. This isn't chili con carne; it's a chili sauce served over spaghetti. Add shredded cheese and there's your three-way. Put onions or red beans on top of that and you've got a four-way. Put them both on top and it's a five-way. This is not the time to be thinking about your arteries.

fronchroom. Chicagoese for front room. The front room is what many of us know as the living room and what used to be called the parlor, from the French *parler*, meaning "to talk." That's what one does in a fronchroom, particularly with guests. So if you're invited to come sit in the fronchroom, don't plan on being a couch potato. There's a social contract to uphold here, in the form of conversation.

fudgies. The name the locals of Michigan's Mackinac Island give the tourists, inspired by the preponderance of fudge shops on the island. Local-lingo giveaway: if you pronounce Mackinac as "Mack-in-ak," you're a fudgie. The locals know it's "Mack-in-aw."

fuss-button. What people in the Midwest have called fussbudgets since at least the 1950s.

gangway. A sidewalk sandwiched between two buildings, but only if you're in Chicago. The more traditional, nautical use of gangway describes a passageway on a ship deck. Both uses suggest a narrow area for traversing, and gangway has always suggested such a confined space.

geez-oh-pete. A variation of "gee whiz" that you're likely to hear in Michigan, Minnesota, and North Dakota. "Jeez" has been around since at least 1920, when it appeared in Sinclair Lewis's *Main Street*, set in Minnesota. "Geez-oh-pete, I can't believe you want to watch *Fargo* for the fifth time."

I'll go with. In much of the Midwest, I don't offer to *go with you*. I simply offer to *go with*. The shorthand is now cropping up in other parts of the country, including Hollywood. The boys of HBO's *Entourage* TV series, which is set in L.A., have been heard to say "I'll come with."

hedge ball. What some in Illinois, Kansas, and other parts of the Midwest have been calling the Osage orange since at least 1890. "Osage" is a Native American word. As for the orange, this is not the kind you're used to snacking on. You can eat the seeds and that's about it. It's been called the hedge-apple, since the plant started off as a living fence—that is, a hedge. The fruit is shaped like a ball, so there you have a hedge ball.

holy buckets. An old-time exclamation of surprise in parts of Minnesota and the Dakotas that you still hear. These are not the buckets used to milk the holy cows, though. These are the raining buckets of the downpour kind.

hoodlebug. A small railroad line that's not much to speak of. Ohioans spoke of hoodlebugs in the 1960s. If you took the **Hoodlebug Express**, you didn't get far or get there very fast.

julebukk. Literally, a Christmas Fool, but in reality, just some Christmas fun. A julebukk arrives at your door between Christmas and New Year's, costumed and masked, seeking some holiday cheer. In other words, hand over the cookies and the drinks. This old Norwegian custom still comes calling in parts of Wisconsin, Minnesota, and North Dakota. It's especially good for those who are no good at caroling but would sure like some hot chocolate.

loosemeat sandwich. Ground beef and onions on a bun, which is known elsewhere as a sloppy joe. It's what you should order in Iowa in particular, as this is the un-patty that the 1990s TV sitcom *Roseanne* popularized. Iowans call it either a loosemeat sandwich or a **tavern sandwich**. Its creator worked in Ye Olde Tavern Sandwich Shop in Sioux City, back in the 1930s.

loper. What people in Michigan's Upper Peninsula call people in the Lower Peninsula. "Loper" is "Lower P," a shortened form of "Lower Peninsula." It doesn't hurt that "loper" is also half of "interloper." We all get a little territorial about those who just come to visit where we've decided to live.

mango pepper. How could the sweet, tropical mango fruit be a pepper? It can't, actually. Mango pepper is another term for bell pepper. Somewhere back in time, "mango" got mangled into meaning something that was pickled, and peppers frequently were (remember Peter Piper). That's the definition of mango in Webster's *Compendious Dictionary* of 1806. Sometimes, in fact, in the Midwest bell peppers are simply called mangoes. So if you bite into one of these thinking it's the fruit, your taste buds will be in a pickle.

pasty. A meat and potato pie. If you're reading this as "paste-ee" (long *a*, as in "ate"), say "past-ee" instead (short *a*, as in "at"). The pasty has a flaky dough that, come to think of it, can look a little pasty (long *a*). But the word is actually Cornish, as pasties originated in

Cornwall, England, before ending up in Michigan's Upper Peninsula.

pickle. Corn Huskers (aka Nebraskans) can smile smugly at this one. They're probably the only ones who will tell you that a pickle is a lottery card. Is that because Nebraskans think you're in a pickle if you lose? Nice try, but no. It's because the tickets used to be sold out of pickle jars. Presumably, this was because the jars were portable and therefore easy to hide away when law enforcement officials showed up in the days before such gambling was legal. Today the language of the state government is peppered with references to these pickles, citing such official legislation as the Nebraska Pickle Card Lottery Act.

please? In Ohio especially, as well as Wisconsin, "please?" often means "pardon me." It's most likely the Germanic influence talking, as *bitte* in German can mean "please repeat again." The joke is how the out-of-towner orders a cheese sandwich in the restaurant, and the waitperson, not hearing what the patron ordered, says "please?" The visitor, not understanding, says "Okay, a cheese sandwich, *please*."

ready for the fox farm. You've had a really bad day and you're ready to pack it all in and call it quits. But you're *just kidding*. Here's why: the real fox farm was where farmers in Minnesota and elsewhere often took their dead or dying animals to be finished off. Back in the 1940s and '50s, fox fur collars were popular for women. The fox farm was a source of this fur. Happily, the fox farms have gone the way of those fur collars.

Ren Cen. Detroit shorthand for the GM Renaissance Center, the city's riverfront complex of skyscrapers.

schnickelfritz. What the German community is likely to affectionately call a little boy full of mischief. Just imagine if those famous rascals of the early days of television had been called the Little Schnickelfritzes.

shirttail relative. One who's distantly related, if that. The expression came on the scene in Kansas in 1927 and was still being heard in Wisconsin in 2001. The shirttail is the afterthought that sometimes hangs out, disconnected from the rest of your clothing. Vermonters have a similar expression: **elbow cousin**. "He's only a shirttail relative, so we barely know him. We're certainly not going to add him to the gift exchange."

side by each. The way some Midwesterners stand side by side. They've been standing this way since at least 1953, particularly in the Germanic communities of Wisconsin. Perhaps the musical that's called *Side by*

Side by Sondheim in the Northeast should be called *Side by Each by Sondheim* in the Midwest.

since Hector was a pup. A long time ago. The unspoken assumption is that Hector hasn't been a pup in years, so that makes whatever it is we're talking about very old indeed. The expression has been around since—well, for a long time. It dates back to 1828, although this puppy didn't get its legs until the early 1900s, when you started hearing it quite often, notably in Indiana and Kansas. "Hector" might have been a reference to the mythical Greek hero of the Trojan War. "Pup" is another way to say someone is young and untried (think of puppy love). "I haven't worn my old uniform since Hector was a pup. I doubt it will fit after all these years."

sliders. Those small, square White Castle hamburgers that just slide down your throat and that Chicagoans are so fond of. The reason they may go down so smoothly is because you're apt to be inhaling them right after the bars close, and you're too tipsy to know any better.

snorkel truck. What Chicagoans are likely to call a fire truck. That's because the Chicago Fire Department created the big-nozzled rigs (hence "snorkel") back in the late 1950s, using tree-trimming trucks as their design inspiration.

the Soo. The nickname for the Upper Peninsula city of Sault Sainte Marie, Michigan. "Soo" is due to Americans' predilection for butchering French, "soo" being the phonetic sound of *sault*. The name harks back to the days of the French fur traders; *sault* is French for rapids or falls, of which the Soo has many.

spider. This will come as news to Miss Muffet, but a spider can also be a frying pan. It's an old-timer term to describe a kind of skillet, or fry pan, that had long "legs" so you could set it over the coals for cooking. The first written recipe that called for a spider was in a nineteenth-century New England cookbook. The term has since traveled to some parts of the South, but also to parts west and north.

sucking hind tit. Getting shoved to the back, and generally being in the loser spot, coming up short. It's what literally happens to the littlest piglet in a litter: it ends up at the back of Mom, sucking on the smallest and skimpiest milk machine. Minnesota farmers find this a useful metaphor for when life sucks (albeit just a little). "We were so late to the party that all the good food was gone, and we ended up sucking hind tit."

Tip-Up Town. A tip-up is the device used in ice fishing that has the little red flag that comes up (tips up) when you have a nibble. On Michigan's Upper Peninsula, so many ice-fishing shanties sprout on the frozen lakes in winter that they turn into Tip-Up Town. It's also known as TUT, but don't look for any Egyptian tombs in this town. TUT has turned into a major winter festival, where the truly brave and foolish take a dip in the icy waters.

Trenary toast. Did you ever wish there were a shorter name for cinnamon-and-sugar toast? Here you go. Trenary is the town in Michigan's Upper Peninsula that made this kind of toast locally famous. You probably add your cinnamon and sugar after the bread's toasted, right? Trenary does just the opposite: the cinnamon and sugar are added before the bread becomes toast.

uff da. What *oy vey* is in Yiddish, *uff da* comes close to being in Norwegian. Among those of Scandinavian descent in Minnesota and other parts of the upper Midwest, "uff da" is an oft-reached-for expression. It can signal surprise, disapproval, disgruntlement—all without cursing or using otherwise questionable words. Try uttering it the next time you stub your toe; it might help.

"Can I Get You a . . . Pop/Tonic/ Soda/Cold Drink/Soft Drink?"

Ask people to tell you what they say here but not there, and the first thing that most pipe up with is soda-not-pop or pop-not-soda. It is the great linguistic divider that unites us. What do *you* call that sweet carbonated beverage you're sipping?

If you're in Cleveland, Indianapolis, Rochester, Buffalo, Detroit, and most of the Midwest, it's **pop**. Why "pop"? Perhaps because of the effervescent quality of this bubbly beverage, which provides a champagne fizz without the alcoholic sparkle.

But pop appears to be getting squashed by **soda**. At the very least, the two have parted company: you used to hear soft drinks referred to as **soda pop** more than you do now, although you'll still hear that in parts of the Mountain West. In most places, it's either/or: soda or pop, not both. And much of the country outside the Midwest drinks soda.

In the Boston area and much of eastern New England, they often get around the whole thing by calling their soft drinks **tonic**. This has a rather medicinal sound. And that, in many ways, goes to the heart of the matter of these beverages.

Back in the 1800s, pharmacists decided to doctor up mineral water, which was considered a curative, with such additions as ginger, sarsaparilla, caffeine, and even coca. (Fittingly, Coca-Cola was invented by a pharmacist, and while today the accent is on the cola, in the beginning it was on the coca.)

These flavored soda waters were soon being dispensed at **soda fountains**, once ubiquitous fixtures inside drugstores. The kid behind the counter who was pulling the levers for the soda water with that jerky motion was called, appropriately, a **soda jerker**. Eventually he became just a **jerk**.

Hence "soda" is what's sipped in much of the East Coast and Southwest. In parts of the South, perhaps as a throwback to those good ol' drugstore days, the beverage is sometimes called **dope**. In certain summertime hot spots such as East Texas, it's called a **cold drink**.

But the generic name for these beverages has become **soft drinks**. Why soft? Because there's no hard liquor in them.

✦

wake me up when the cows come home. A positive way of saying don't wake me up for anything, unless I'm a Minnesota dairy farmer and the cows have come home from their pastures. That's when they turn into money machines, provided you're there to milk them. It's worth waking up for even if you're dog tired, but nothing else is.

Woodstock for Capitalists. Unlike the original Woodstock, which happened only in 1969, this gathering takes place every year in Omaha, when über-capitalist, investor guru, and local boy Warren Buffett convenes the annual shareholder meeting of his company, Berkshire Hathaway. Who needs drugs when you can get high on owning a share of the same stock as the **Oracle of Omaha**? (That would be Warren.)

Yoopers. If you've been to Michigan's Finn-filled Upper Peninsula, you know it's inhabited with Yoopers. The term is what happens when you say "U-P-ers" quickly, U-P being Upper Peninsula.

✹
Strip Tease

Between the sidewalk and the street in many a residential neighborhood is a patch of grass whose main purpose is to welcome the garbage cans on trash day. Civil engineers know it as an easement. For some reason this boring little strip of not-much gets some interesting local-lingo treatment.

Akron, Youngstown, and other parts of northeastern Ohio win the prize for most distinctive name with **devil's strip**. First recorded in 1957, the term is presumably what a judge in a civil case called this no-man's-land between what the homeowner is responsible for and the city is in charge of.

The devil is much mellower in Tennessee, where this grassy patch becomes the **neutral strip**. Bonackers call it **neutral ground**, which in Louisiana and southern Mississippi is more likely to be the name for the median of a divided roadway.

Parkway is the name Midwesterners are apt to call the strip, while in western New York, it's the **subway**. Minnesotans give it the grand name of **boulevard**.

New York City residents call it a **tree lawn**, perhaps in the hopes that by naming it such, green will magically appear in the pavement. (Well, they did get a tree to grow in Brooklyn.)

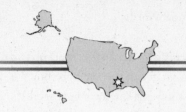

BLUE NORTHERS
AND LOST BREAD

Texas and Louisiana

Why single out these two states? Their unique histories, primarily.

Texas was first part of Mexico and then its own republic before it became a state, and it was more or less bilingual. Within its vast borders Spanish, Southern, and cowboy vernacular have plenty of room to roam.

While much of the eastern and southern United States draws on an Anglo-Scots-Irish heritage for its earliest days, Louisiana's is French. Even today, there are no counties in Louisiana; instead, there are parishes. This is the land of both Creole and Cajun, the place where English meets French meets African, with some Spanish and Choctaw thrown into the stew—make that jambalaya.

all hat and no cattle. Said of someone who's an impostor or a poseur. Anyone can put on a cowboy hat, but that doesn't mean the person knows how to rustle cattle—metaphorically and otherwise speaking. If Jay Gatsby had gone to West Texas rather than to West Egg, Nick Carraway would have eventually found him out to be not so great after all, but just all hat and no cattle.

alligator pear. Avocado by a more colorful Louisiana name. All kinds of complicated theories abound as to how this name came about. It might be just this simple: an avocado is shaped like a pear (as Bartlett's *Dictionary of Americanisms* indicated in 1859), and the bumpy skin of an avocado calls to mind the alligator's hide. The expression was first recorded in America in 1766, in Florida. Both Louisiana and Florida have the kind of steamy swamps that gators like to hang out in, making these reptiles all too familiar to the residents. (*Avocado* was a word in early Spanish, but it meant "lawyer"—what's now *abogado*.)

between hay and grass. Not yet a man, no longer just a boy. This is a peripatetic expression, following the east-to-west path of many earlier Americans. Nantucket was where they said it first—or at least, recorded it—in 1848. Next it was heard in New York and Connecticut. By 1933 it had reached the Ozarks. Now it seems, for the most part, to have settled in Texas and farther west.

"He just turned fifteen, and he's reached that stage where he's between hay and grass."

blue norther. The north wind that blows ill with chill in Texas. Most likely it started out as a "blew-tailed norther" among cattle drivers back in the 1850s. The segue from "blew" to "blue" might have been because of the blue-black color of the clouds that come up. Blue also suggests the color folks turn if they're caught off guard in this wind, as temperatures can plummet. But blue barely scratches the colorful language found among Texans. They don't stop at just naming their winds. They tell you just how windy it is, as this description found in *Texas Monthly* attests: "The wind's **blowing like perfume through a prom.**"

brake tag. The sticker you get when your car is inspected, if it's being inspected in New Orleans. Since you don't have to drive too far there to drive into water, you want those brakes to work. Floridians don't have such stickers, but they do have a **tag**, which most everyone else knows as a license plate.

cedar robe. You're apt to find such a fragrant item in Louisiana and Mississippi, and no, it's not the kind of robe you wrap yourself up in after a bath. The cedar robe is a closet, but a freestanding one. The "robe" is short for "wardrobe," a cabinet or cupboard built to hold garments—actually, to guard them, as the Old French *warder*, "to guard," is the root. Cedar does indeed guard against moths and other pesky, drawn-to-cloth critters.

cowbelly. Ever feel a cow's stomach? Save yourself the trouble. It feels like soft river mud. That's what they've been calling this mud in Louisiana, at least since the 1950s. You also sometimes hear people talk about **putting their cowbellies on**—meaning the boots they wear when slogging through the cowbelly.

dirty rice. A Cajun rice dish that involves chicken gizzards, and therefore gives the rice a brownish tinge. That's your so-called dirt.

fait-do-do. Depending on how you wish to read it, "fait-do-do" means either "go to sleep" or "let's party with some Cajun dancing." Say "fay doe doe" and you'll sound a wee bit Cajun—*oui?* The expression is rooted in French, the language as essential to Cajun as okra is to gumbo. The Cajuns are descendants of the eighteenth-century French settlers who were booted out of Acadia in Nova Scotia, Canada, and ended up in southwest Louisiana. (The word "Cajun" derives from "Acadia.") *Fait* is French for "to make"; "do-do" harks back to *dormir*, "to sleep." So how do you go from sleeping, one meaning of the expression, to fait-do-do's other meaning about dancing? One explanation is that Cajun moms urge their little ones to lay themselves down to sleep, so that Mom can go kick up her heels dancing. It certainly adds spice to the expression, which is sometimes spelled "fais-dodo."

fart-knocker. A bad fall from a horse—the kind that can take the wind right out of you. Thank cowboy lore for the term.

first cousin to Moses Rose. There is no more cowardly a coward in Texas lore than Louis Moses Rose. He was the only one to skedaddle from the Alamo before the final battle. If a Texan ever describes you in this manner, know you've been deeply insulted. "He turned and ran the minute he smelled trouble—you would've thought he was first cousin to Moses Rose."

go-cup. A disposable cup you can get only in New Orleans. It holds liquor—even if you can't—when you want to take your drink from the bar out to the street. "I'll have a scotch on the rocks with a splash of vermouth, and put it in a go-cup, please."

go-go. Your butt, in French Louisiana. Don't fall on your go-go, as it may be hard to get up-up.

don't put the gris-gris on me. Don't put a hex or a spell on me. "Gris-gris" is how a Frenchman back in the 1700s heard the local Africans in Louisiana refer to the charms they used to channel the spell. Gris-gris can, at times, be a good spell, but it's not advisable to assume such.

G.T.T. "Gone to Texas." This nineteenth-century acronym seems simple enough, given the many people who hitched their wagon to the Lone Star back then. But it also became a kind of code to indicate a lowlife or otherwise questionable fellow. You could use the expression, therefore, as either noun or verb. "He's a G.T.T., so watch out for him," a lawman might say. And when the long arm of the law couldn't reach a wanted man, the report would often read simply, "G.T.T."

hair in the butter. Texas talk for a sensitive issue. Try neatly removing one hair from a stick of butter and you'll get it (the expression, not necessarily the hair). A later usage of the phrase is to suggest skepticism: a 1980 article in the *Houston Chronicle* maintained that in East Texas, if you're questioning something, you say there's a hair in the butter.

she threw a hissy. Hissy is Texan for tantrum—at least, Texas is where they said it first. Now throughout the South, someone might be said to **pitch a hissy fit**. Such a nerved-up Nelly is near "hysterical," the word that started hissy.

hitched but not churched. Said in Texas of a couple who are living like they're married even though they're not.

K&B purple. How some New Orleanians say purple. The color purple there evokes not a movie or a book but the ubiquitous purple of the old K&B drugstores, a local chain that got swallowed up by a national one.

lost bread. French toast. In New Orleans, no food is ever really lost; it's just repurposed. When you have old bread that's so stale it's—to use the popular slang expression—toast, you make French toast out of it. "Lost bread" is actually a literal translation, or calque, of the French *pain perdu* (*pain* is pronounced like "pen").

making groceries. How you do your grocery shopping in New Orleans. But here you don't *do*, you *make*. Thank that French heritage. "Making groceries" is from the French *faire le marché*, which literally means "to make the market."

may you never get your spurs tangled. A good-luck wish from the Old West.

Mister Go. That's how New Orleanians pronounce MRGO, the acronym for the Mississippi River–Gulf Outlet navigation canal. It was dug in the 1960s as a shortcut from the Gulf of Mexico to the harbor of New Orleans.

pirooting. People caught pirooting are often nosing around. The word is what happens when Americans twirl the French word *pirouette* around on their tongues, something we started doing as early as 1858. To pirouette is to twirl around. Both Louisianans and Texans have been known to do it.

put the grip up in the locker. Put the suitcase away in the closet, if you're in Louisiana. Just don't confuse this grip with **grippe**, which means the flu.

rid hard and put up wet. Texan for exhausted, after a long day in the saddle.

you'll do to ride the river with. You're loyal and dependable enough to cross a treacherous river with. Eric Clapton sang about this, Louis L'Amour wrote about it, and the TV series *Walker, Texas Ranger* devoted an episode to it. Take is as a high compliment if a Texan says this to you. The expression harks back to the days when cowboys had to herd their cattle across dangerous rivers. When the saying first made it into print, in 1940, the river in question was the Rio Grande.

round ass. A coward, in cowboy vernacular. How so? Because he's gone soft and won't ride a bucking horse. Try goading someone you have a dare with by telling him or her not to be a round ass.

scared as a sinner in a cyclone. You can't get much scareder than this. If you as a sinner perish in a cyclone (good odds), guess where you're going next? Hint: it's a place even **hotter than a tamale**, as a Texan might say about hell.

Schwegmann's bag. A large size. Schwegmann Brothers Giant Super Markets, once the landmark local grocery store chain in New Orleans (it was sold in the late 1990s), used to have humongous brown paper bags. They became a local measuring stick for big. "That purse you're carrying is like a Schwegmann's bag. I could put my lunch inside and I swear there'd still be room for the kitchen sink."

shoo-shoo. A failed firecracker in Louisiana—what some in Pennsylvania call a **hisser**. "Shoo-shoo" calls to mind "susurrus" in more than just sound, for "whisper" is another meaning of both "shoo-shoo" and "susurrus." In her 1935 book *Mules and Men*, Zora Neale Hurston wrote, "Lucy and Ella were alternately shoo-shooing to each other and guffawing." This kind of a whisper has the rustling of gossip to it.

shoot-da-chute. What some kids in Louisiana call the playground slide. "Chute" is another word for a steep incline, as on a slide, which you shoot down.

they'd steal the nickels off a dead man's eyes. Whoever would do this is an unscrupulous lowlife, a person lacking morals and conscience. This Texpression alludes to Greek mythology and the Greek custom of placing coins in the eyes of the deceased. The coins served as payment for the ferryman to transport the dead person safely across the Styx, the river that separated the living from the dead. The Greeks coughed up considerably more than nickels, but nevertheless, the sentiment is the same.

You Say Hello . . .

Globalization goes only so far. You can still spot Americans abroad by using your ears instead of your eyes: they're the ones who say "hi" as a form of greeting. Its linguistic ancestry is older than Columbus, being a variant of "Hy!," an exclamation used in the Old World back in 1475. The first American to say "hi" instead of "hello"—or at least, the first one recorded—was a Kansan, in 1862. That makes it an American word by just a year: Kansas was granted statehood in January 1861.

"Hi" is within linguistic shouting distance of **hey**, which made it into Webster's *Compendious Dictionary* of 1806 as "a word of joy or exhortation." We're usually glad to see the person we're greeting, so that's the joy part of it. As for the exhortation—if you heard someone in Missouri shout **hi there** in 1892, that person was most likely trying to herd cows.

"Hey" hewed to its exclamatory nature through the nineteenth century, particularly in the Midwest and Southwest. A Californian in 1899 said, "Well, it's a go then, hey?"

As a greeting, "hey" is more Southern and dates back to at least the 1930s. "Tell him hey for me," says a character in *To Kill a Mockingbird*. Another Alabaman, baseball legend Willie Mays, was nicknamed the Say Hey Kid in the 1950s for his way of greeting folks. **Hey, how you?** inquires the South Carolinian.

"How do you do" started as early as 1697. (Does *anybody* say that anymore?) From "how do you do," it's barely a linguistic hop to "how-d'ye," *ye* being an old form of *you*. Say "how-d'ye" fast and you have **howdy**.

Americans got a hankering for "howdy" in the mid-1800s. It may sound Western today but it started off in the South, where it was a common greeting by the end of the Civil War. Even back then, Americans exhibited that penchant to verbify, and they'd turn "howdy" into a verb, as when they said in Kentucky, **we've howdy'd but not shook**. In Florida, a burrowing owl known for its vigorous bobs of the head is sometimes called the **howdy owl**.

"Howdy" and "hi" occasionally get together, as when the Texan says **hidy**, the Californian says **hidy-doody**, or the Alabaman says **hidy-do**. No wonder Americans are often characterized as friendly—we have so many greetings. But "greeting" didn't always mean what we think it does. In the 1960s and '70s, you might hear **greeting** used jokingly in Georgia and Tennessee to mean subpoena. (Your mother *told* you not to talk to strangers.)

But—*hello-o-o*, you say, what about "hello"? It comes from a French term for "stop," the way you'd say it if you were trying to hail a carriage. A version of hail-as-hello could be heard in the 1940s along the outer Northeastern coast, primarily Long Island, Cape Cod, and Maine. Instead of saying "call me," you'd say **give me a hail**. **Hello May**, which a Southerner or Southwesterner might say, was a gentle damnation popular in the 1960s that suggested "Hail Mary."

Americans started saying "hello" in the 1860s. As a way to show surprise, people in the Midwest were exclaiming "hello!" back in 1917. Today we might say "whaddup" or "zup" and think we're cool, but our ancestors were saying **what's up** as early as the 1880s.

What's new and **whadda you know** are New Yorkisms, as is **how's by you**. **Shalom aleichem** is a Yiddish greeting, meaning "peace unto you." The rejoinder, **aleichem shalom** ("and unto you, peace") is also a way to say farewell.

Most of us say "good-bye" in one form or another. The word was just catching on when the Pilgrims were saying good-bye to all that in Europe. It was a contraction of "God be with you." In Appalachia, a plant that blooms in the fall is called a **good-bye-summer**. In Arkansas, an aftertaste is known as a **goodbye-taste**. And in Georgia, someone found another way to say "hearse" in 1969: **good-bye wagon**.

suck the head, squeeze the tip. Nothing to do with sucking face or whatever else along those lines you may be thinking. It's how you eat crawfish, brought to you by those in Louisiana, who eat plenty of 'em. And if somebody here offers to cook you some **mud bugs**, say yes. That's just another name for the crawfish, aka crayfish.

Texas stomp. Some know it as a kind of line dance, but it's also what you call a vigorous foot-crunching of a plastic water jug when you're flattening it for the recycling bin. Everything's bigger in Texas, remember, including the force with which you can flatten a plastic bottle.

tighter than bark off a tree. Stingy as can be. Just try peeling bark off most healthy trees and you'll see why the saying works.

yat. The way "where y'at?" comes out when New Orleanians say it. Drop the "where" and keep just the "yat." But they're not asking you where you are. "Yat" is as familiar a saying here as "how ya doing" and "hey there" are elsewhere. The phrase probably got its start in a blue-collar section of the city upriver from the French Quarter known as the Irish Channel. Now it's one of those cool insider words that everybody wants to use. (Note to visitors: as to where you're at in the city, you're upriver or down, downtown or up, but never on something like East Thirty-third Street. There are just too many colorful street names in New Orleans to bother with east, west, north, and south.)

What to Say If You're Dead

We Americans have a number of lively ways to say "dead." **Dropped off** is one way to say it in Appalachia. (The rest of us use a watered-down version to refer to someone whom we haven't seen in ages—someone who's dropped off the face of the earth.) **Standing in the drop-edge of yonder** is how you're likely to hear it said in Tennessee. **All anymore** is what the Pennsylvania Dutch have said since at least 1859, or simply **all**, as if to say, "She's all gone."

Buck out, say Westerners, with a nod to the doings of the cowboys and their bucking, kicking animals. **Kick off** is another such Westernism, although this can be heard in the Midwest as well.

Once you're in the **misty beyond** (more cowboy-speak, this time from Idaho), they're apt to put you in a **bone orchard**—aka cemetery. Contrast that earthy orchard with the kind some Northerners head to, the **marble orchard**—inspired, of course, by all those marble headstones and crypts. In Boontling, the funeral is the **croaking**, reminiscent of the slang "to croak," or die. "Croak" was slang as early as 1812, an onomatopoeic way to describe what the death rattle sounded like.

Death has a certain self-serve quality in the Ozarks. **You dig your grave with a fork and spoon**, they say—a bouncier way to say "you are what you eat." **I like to die**, say Southerners, even though they don't enjoy it one bit. They're simply saying, "I thought I'd die."

If you do die, the old cowboy talk would say you **got a halo gratis**, and the boys would **put you to bed with a pick and shovel**, another take on the idea of digging your own grave. If the person doing the digging is Texan, he's just **opened himself up a worm farm**.

There goes hoss and beaver, lament the old mountain men from the Rockies—the horse and the beaver being among the few living creatures these trappers would see. He's **finished his circle**, says the old cowhand.

He's **bought the farm**, maintains the Ozarks mourner. The expression is heard in other parts of the country as well, and it may be one of the linguistic legacies of World War II. (Either that or it's a really good not-so-urban legend worth perpetuating.) Many of the military personnel, particularly air force, either hailed from a farm or spoke about buying themselves one when they retired. The government issued life insurance policies for the soldiers. If they were killed, the insurance money could be used to pay off the mortgage on the farm. Thus, the dead soldiers bought the farm. The equation of farm (grave) with soldiers dates back even earlier, signifying the last bit of land a soldier could call his own.

Those who've bought the farm have **turned up their toes**, another Ozarks expression, and gone to **Boot Hill**. This frontier term for cemetery was inspired by the fact that many of its rough-and-ready residents really did die with their boots on.

But it's not just the West where footwear plays a part in having one's foot in the grave. **Hanging up your boots** is heard among old-timers in Maine, where rubber boots are a common sight near the sea. He **coiled his ropes**, these same folks are apt to say of a shipmate who has died, alluding to the tidying a seaman would do on board before leaving the ship.

She's **going over in her book** is another Maine expression, meaning she's not yet dead but is getting darn close. She'll **peg out** is another northern New England expression, anticipating the same.

And when she does, the Southerner will announce that she **passed**, a more laconic way of saying "passed away." It's how Shakespeare himself would have said it—and did: "Disturb him not; let him pass peaceably" (*Henry VI, Part II*).

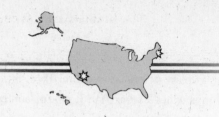

THAT'S ABOVE
MY BEND

The Southwest and California

Granted, combining Northern and Southern California into the same chapter is a bit like putting the Northern and Southern Hemispheres together and calling them Cleveland. Similarly, Santa Fe and Albuquerque can seem as different as San Francisco and Santa Cruz. But residents of California and the Southwest do have in common that talent for venturing farther—whether they be cowboy, prospector, or venture capitalist.

above my bend. A Western way to say that something is a bit beyond your abilities. The phrase was first recorded in Tennessee in 1835 but then headed west around the bend. For this "bend," go back to "bent" as a noun, and its meaning of disposition or inclination.

air the lungs. Cussing, cowboy style. Where there were cowboys swearing in the West, there was much airing of the lungs, since at least 1911, when "air the lungs" first aired to ears making note of it.

air the paunch. Vomiting, cowboy style. From this meaning, recorded in 1920, came a second meaning heard just eight years later: to brag. Think about it— don't folks who are always bragging on themselves sometimes make you want to throw up?

all down but nine. Someone who's not too with it. The allusion is to bowling, where the object is to knock down all ten pins. The surprise is that the expression is linked to the Old West. (They *bowled*? Who knew?) Mark Twain used the phrase in his 1872 travel memoir of Nevada and other points west, *Roughing It*.

Arizona nightingale. A donkey in the Southwest. Ever heard a donkey bray? Sounds just like a nightingale. Remember, this is the desert, where mirages are common. They've been singing this tune about donkeys and nightingales since at least 1940. Hey, it's better than listening to an ARIZONA TENOR.

Arizona tenor. That's desert-speak for the consumptive with a tubercular cough. Back in the 1940s, before Arizona became deluged with humidity-raising swimming pools, its bone-dry climate was considered sauna-soothing for the lungs. Many an Arizona tenor hoped the dry air would cure the cough.

buckaroo. A cowboy, West Coast style. Thank the Spanish influence, particularly in California, for this swaggering-sounding word. It's what happened when the Spanish *vaquero* found its way onto American tongues, which it did at least by the 1920s. The *v* in Spanish is sometimes pronounced like a *b*. *Vaca* is Spanish for cow.

burn the breeze. To ride fast, and that originally meant on a horse. Now it applies to horseless carriages—aka cars—as well.

the Burque. What many Burqueños affectionately call their city. Can you guess which city? It's Albuquerque, which was originally spelled Alburquerque. Several years ago some lawmakers tried to get the spelling changed back to the original, but no luck. "The Burque," on the other hand, needs no official blessing, and sometimes it's a way that Burqueños thumb their noses at those who think it would be cool to call the city "the Q."

California prayer book. Don't look for one of these in any church. This was the euphemism that the unholy high rollers from Gold Rush days gave to a deck of cards. This form of worship, first heard in 1851, was still going strong during the Civil War.

chesterfield. A couch, in a slice of Northern California. Californians probably got the word from the Canadians, who may well have swiped it from the English, where lived the Earl of Chesterfield. The word is seldom heard now when "sofa" or "couch" will do, but furniture sellers still use "chesterfield" to describe a large leather couch.

chew it finer. Say it plainer. From the days when those plain-speaking cowboys came out with their colorful expressions.

Christmas style. How you can have almost any dish—breakfast, lunch, or dinner—in New Mexico. Pair red chile sauce with green chile sauce, and you have the colors of Christmas. "Make those eggs Christmas style, please."

coyote. This cunning prairie wolf has come to signify a sneaky, underhanded person. But in California and Texas, "coyote" has taken on an even more sinister meaning. Someone who smuggles people across the border from Mexico for far more money than the people have is such a coyote.

desert canary. A burro in the cowboy West. When a burro bellows its loud bray, close your eyes and you could swear you're listening to a canary (uh-huh). The book *Cowboy Lingo*, published in 1936, makes the distinction between burros and mules this way: burros are desert canaries and mules are hard tails. Another taxonomic tip: a donkey is an ass, a burro is a little ass, and a mule (which is a donkey-horse hybrid) is a half-ass. A canary is just a canary.

dime-a-dip dinner. A fund-raising ploy begun in the 1950s, whereby you pay ten cents for each item of food you want. How ironic that the land of high rollers, Nevada, is where dime-a-dip first made its appearance in print, in the late 1960s. Originally the dime-a-dips were benefits for the Mormon faith, but now lots of religious and nonprofit groups believe in their fund-raising powers. The expression has found its way into Sue Grafton's *F Is for Fugitive* mystery: "He'd met Oribelle, en route, at a dime-a-dip dinner at a Baptist church in Fayetteville, Arkansas."

don't that take the rag off the bush. Don't that beat all! Something is either outstanding or outrageous if it takes the rag off the bush. This happens mainly in the West and the South, although parts of the Midwest exclaim in this fashion, too. It started as early as 1810. One explanation: people used to hang their washing on hedges, or bushes, to dry. Someone swiping one of their "rags," or clothing items, would be pretty outrageous.

earthquake weather. Humid, hot, and no wind. What the South knows as summer, in other words. But in California, they view such sticky-icky conditions as the first possible rumblings of an earthquake. The term has been around since 1865.

Emerald Triangle. Mendocino, Humboldt, and Trinity counties in California. North Carolina may have the Research Triangle Park of businesses, and Boston may boast the Emerald Necklace of parkways, but only California could have an Emerald Triangle. It consists of these three northern counties, and it refers to the area's major cash crop: marijuana. (It's legal in California, within limits, to grow medical marijuana.)

go-aheads. That's flip-flops to most everyone else, but in California and Hawaii, you'll often hear those toe-gripping strips of sandals called by this name. One theory for the name is that you can walk right out of go-aheads and your feet still keep going ahead. The term was first recorded in the 1960s and was inspired by the Japanese *zori*, the more substantial sandal with the separator for the big toe. Go ahead and call those flip-flops by this other name. It's best, however, to refrain from calling them what an earlier generation did: **thongs**. That word has taken on a whole new meaning in the lingerie department.

Hangtown fry. Hang on to your arteries. This omelet-on-steroids consists of fried eggs, breaded oysters, and bacon. Back in the mid-1800s, at the height of California's Gold Rush fever, this was the most expensive meal a lucky miner could order. Hangtown was where they first concocted it. The town's name has since changed to Placerville, but the Hangtown fry name stayed. Some restaurants have recently revived the dish. You might have to revive your arteries after they get a Hangtown fry.

Hassayamper. An old-timer, or a liar. The term was minted in Arizona during the Gold Rush days. Legend had it that those who drank from the Hassayampa River near Phoenix would never again speak the truth. The word then became the West's version of Caesar's famous crossing of the Rubicon. In this case, "to cross the Hassayampa River" meant you no longer knew how to tell the truth. The expression was first recorded in 1927; the head of the American Bar Association used it in a speech. We'll make no comment about lawyers and drinking the water.

Hollywood 8. The most prominent top teeth, and ergo the ones most likely to get capped if you're a Hollywood star (or just want to smile like one). Start with your two front teeth and fan out in each direction till you count four on both sides. Guess where this expression originated. It seems that ever since there's been Movieland, there's been talk about teeth. In 1936 the composer George Gershwin, who was living in Hollywood at the time, wrote excitedly to a friend about a party being held for the writer Moss Hart. Over a hundred people came. The occasion? Hart's new teeth.

Hosteen. In the Navajo language, *Hastqin* is a term of respect for a man (rather like addressing him as "Mister"). So when someone in Arizona or New Mexico says "Hey, Hosteen," meaning "Hey, old man," the person is showing respect.

It's It. In San Francisco, it's the ice cream sandwich that became a local favorite ever since its inventor, George Whitney, sandwiched vanilla ice cream between two oatmeal cookies and dipped it in dark chocolate. That was back in 1928, and for years it was available only at the amusement park Whitney owned. Now its fame has spread farther afield. As for its name—the story goes that Whitney hollered "It's it" when he hit his eureka moment. Not very original, but it'll do.

lay the dust. How cowboys took a drink when they were parched. A drink that lay the dust was one that banished all the dirt in your throat from the trail.

make the riffle. To succeed, California style. They've been heard to be making the riffle (or sometimes, the ripple) since at least 1853. Some folks say the gold miners coined the term, since riffle is part of the sluice that miners used to find gold nuggets. Others say piffle to that origin of "riffle": it has to do with mastering the rapids, since that's another meaning of riffle. "I think it's fair to say that the Apple iPad makes the riffle."

peewees. The only time you should use this term when talking with a New Mexico cattleman is if you're admiring his handsome, short-top boots. Those boots used to be higher, but in the early 1900s a few practical-minded cowboys whacked off their high-tops after their boots got ripped up in roping competitions. Peewees have been the fashion ever since.

piker. A good-for-nothing, and furthermore, a shiftless cheapskate and a small-time gambler. Piker is a California put-down dating back to the Gold Rush days of the nineteenth century, recorded as early as 1854. A whole bunch of gold diggers from Pike County, Missouri, went west to find their fortune, since they were mighty poor farmers. Their poor ways made an unfavorable impression among the other gold diggers, and the pejorative term stuck.

pogonip. A dense, chilly, winter fog that you encounter in the mountains of Nevada and parts of California. The term is Shoshonean, first recorded in 1865. No doubt the locals couldn't find any other words to describe this heavy and often relentless cold blanket of air.

WATERLESS WORDS FOR WATER

Water, water everywhere—except in these words, all of which have something to do with H_2O. See if you can match the word with where you're most likely to hear it.

1. **HOLE**—a small harbor
2. **BRANCH**—a stream
3. **HOUSE**—a Swamp Thing word, meaning a clump of bushes and trees that are on land above water level

4. **HUMMOCK**—more Swamp Thing: similar to a house, except that the vegetation is a grove of large trees
5. **BOGUE**—a river that walks rather than runs
6. **COULEE**—a bayou, or small stream, that often dries up in summer
7. **TANK**—a watering hole for cattle
8. **GUT**—a small waterway that connects to larger ones
9. **CHUCK**—a harbor
10. **KILL**—a stream

ANSWERS

1. **HOLE:** New England and Virginia. Woods Hole, for example, is a small village on Cape Cod with a harbor. Local-lingo note: not all holes are the H_2O variety. The hole in Jackson Hole, for instance, indicates a mountain valley. What these two holes have in common is that they dip. *Hole* is the Old English word that gave us "hollow."
2. **BRANCH:** the South. As early as 1624, a Virginia history described a river dividing into branches.
3. **HOUSE:** Georgia. More specifically, the Okefenokee Swamp. These portions of dry land offer a certain shelter for both hunters of swamp life and creatures of the swamp such as deer. Thus there's a place to house them, an expression first recorded in the 1920s.
4. **HUMMOCK:** Florida. It's sometimes spelled "hammock" and has nothing to do with the kind you swing in, except that both are elevated. Explorers to America used the term as far back as 1589.
5. **BOGUE:** Louisiana. The word meanders all the way back to the region's native Choctaws, who called a river a *bok*.
6. **COULEE:** Louisiana and parts of Mississippi. The word is from the French for "to flow," so it's not sur-

prising you'd hear it here. Midwesterners maintain that land can flow just as much as water, though, which is why the valleys of southern Wisconsin are sometimes described as "coulee country." Go farther west and those gently sloping valleys turn into deep gullies that go by the same name.

7. TANK: Texas. "Tank" as a source of drinking water dates back to the seventeenth century. It's a word the Portuguese swiped from India.

8. GUT: Delmarva—aka the parts of Delaware, Maryland, and Virginia that share the Chesapeake Bay. "Gut" was recorded in Virginia back in 1636, when it was spelled "gutt." Guts are often named for someone. There's Emma's Gut in Delaware and Ben's Gut in Maryland. The word probably started out as the old Dutch *gote*, for drain or gutter.

9. CHUCK: Alaska and the Pacific Northwest. This Chinook word was first recorded in 1899, in a U.S. Fish and Wildlife Service bulletin for Alaska. If "chuck" means harbor, what would *saltchuck* mean? Right: the ocean.

10. KILL: parts of New York State, including the Catskills. *Kil* is Dutch for "stream" and is a vestige of the early days when the Dutch laid claim to New York (then New Amsterdam). So the town of Fishkill has nothing to do with killing fish, nor Kaaterskill Falls with killing kaaters.

rusher. Someone who's in an all-fire hurry to stake a claim in an area newly opened to settlers. There would seem to be no such areas left—and yet look at how many rushers there were to the Sun Belt in recent years.

sachet kitten. From the land that gave us sex kittens comes a far less appealing creature. Sachet kitten is a Californiaism for skunk, first recorded in 1921.

Taos lightning. Whiskey that packs a powerful wallop. Taos lightning was brewed at a mill near—wait for it—Taos, New Mexico, back in the early days of trappers and mountain men. It's possible that the liquor appeared before the name, which flashed onto the horizon in the 1850s. Another name at the time for this particular whiskey was **mountain dew**.

te watcho. A little bit of L.A. Spanglish here. It can mean "I'm looking out (for you)" or "watch out for yourself."

totally tubular. California-born surfer slang for "excellent," inspired by the way the surf curls into a giant tube that is the perfect wave.

zanja. Another word we swiped from the Spanish, as it sounds a whole lot nicer than "ditch," which is what it means. Not the kind of ditch you fall into but the kind where water flows to where it's needed—like the old Roman aqueducts. The Zanja Madre, or Mother Ditch, is how L.A. got its water back in pueblo days.

THE BEER STOPS HERE

Once upon a time in America you could figure out where folks were from by the name of the beer they drank. Can you guess where you probably would have been at the beginning of the twentieth century if you were drinking this brand of beer?

1. Anchor Steam
2. Blatz
3. Carling
4. Falstaff
5. Hamm's
6. Iron City
7. Narragansett
8. Olympia
9. Pabst
10. Shiner

ANSWERS AND BREWERY FOUNDING DATES

1. San Francisco, 1896
2. Milwaukee, 1846
3. Cleveland, 1898
4. Saint Louis, 1870
5. Saint Paul, 1865
6. Pittsburgh, 1861
7. Rhode Island, 1890
8. Pacific Northwest, 1896
9. Milwaukee, 1844
10. Texas, 1909

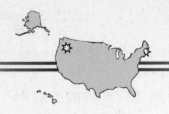

SPENDY

The Mountains, Northwest, and Pacific Northwest

"The cowards never started and the weak died on the way," goes the old saying about those who ventured west—or not—on the Oregon Trail in the mid-1800s. Here is the land of loggers and ranchers, mountain ranges and Mormon faith—and also of Starbucks, Amazon, and Microsoft.

appleknocker. Elsewhere this person might be known as a rube or a hick, but in the Northwest, where fruit is ripe for the picking, such a rustic has been an appleknocker since the early 1900s. The term suggests a certain pecking order as far as manual labor. Experienced loggers would call someone who'd just arrived on the job an appleknocker. Seasoned miners in Montana and Idaho would do the same when describing those new on the job. A comparable derogatory term was **alfalfa pickers**. "Appleknocker" was doubly insulting once you figured out that those who do harvest apples don't actually knock them off the trees.

a barbed-wire deal. A thorny situation. The loggers of the Pacific Northwest have been known to say this. Such a raw deal has been around since the 1950s.

bar pit. It might sound like a beer joint that's a dive, but this bar pit is actually the drainage ditch that runs alongside a road. Okay, that explains "pit," but what's up with the "bar"? That's "borrow" with a slight drawl. A borrow pit in the world of civil engineers is where you take fill from one location to use in another—you borrow from Peter to fill Paul. So a drainage ditch becomes a de facto borrow, or bar, pit. It has been so since at least 1949, when the term was first recorded in Colorado. In Oklahoma, they ditch the pit and just call it a **bar ditch**.

don't bogart that. Don't hog whatever "that" is. This West Coast slang started in the 1960s, and its point of reference was how Humphrey Bogart would always have a cigarette in his mouth. Those who did that with a marijuana cigarette were hogging the joint rather than sharing it. So if you're hoarding something, or stealing something like an idea, you're bogarting it. Which means, as Lauren Bacall once said to Bogie in one of their films, you're a stinker.

branded-in-the-hide. True-blue, dyed-in-the-wool, Western style. Those Westerners who've raised cattle have a long history of branding hides, so they know how strongly it sticks. It's in contrast to **brand artist**, basically a con artist with cattle: someone who steals cattle and changes the true owner's brand markings. Marketers, meanwhile, long ago swiped the term "brand" to signify an entity's true-blue identity.

let's go to the coast. On the East Coast it's beaches, or in places like Jersey, the shore. And around Baltimore, they go "down-nee-ocean." But on the West Coast, Oregon especially, you don't go to the beach or the shore or nee-ocean: you go to the coast. Even the mountain range that goes along this part of the west coast is called the Coast Range.

Colorado Kool-Aid. Three guesses what this one means. Yes, it's a Coloradan nickname for Coors beer, a Colorado creation started in 1873. You heard this more when Coors was a local drink, before it went national beginning in the early 1990s.

culinary water. The only kind you want to drink in Utah: it's Utah-ese for potable water. They've been calling it culinary since at least 1883.

don't know sic 'em from come here. A long way of saying that somebody's stupid. Somebody was smart enough to record the phrase back in the early 1900s. It means you don't know diddly about whatever the topic is. A parallel phrase is **not worth sic 'em.** In other words, it's worthless.

fourteener. A mountain higher than fourteen thousand feet. Colorado can lay claim to the expression, as it has more than fifty fourteeners. (California and Alaska are runners-up.) The word has been around for centuries among poets, as it indicates fourteen syllables in a line or fourteen lines in a poem—what's often known as a sonnet.

fry sauce. Utah's famous condiment for french fries. Don't ask for anything but when you're in Utah or they'll know you're not from here. Invented by a local restaurateur in the late 1940s, fry sauce is a mix of mayo and ketchup and various spices.

geoduck. Say "gooey duck" and you'll sound like you're from the Puget Sound area where this mother-of-all-mollusks is found. The largest clam in the world—it can get to be nine pounds—it's more chewy than gooey. It won't win any beauty contests, but if your neck (siphon) was seven times as long as the rest of you, you wouldn't be so fetching, either. Nevertheless, this Pacific clam shows up its punier Atlantic rival, the **quahog**, in larger-than-life Western style. The term is Native American and means "dig deep," as the clam burrows deep. Shellfish lovers, dig in.

go-dig. A tool used in cultivating crops. What you go dig with, in other words, at least if you're digging in Colorado. If you're in Missouri, you might call this same tool a **snake-killer**.

half a bubble off plumb. If something is crooked on a carpenter's level, it's half a bubble off. Portland, Oregon, was the first place to apply this carpenter's expression, in 1982. It's come to mean someone who's a little ditsy . . . not playing with a full deck . . . who has a few screws loose . . . is half a bubble off plumb.

hooky bobbing. When it's snowing out and you grab on to the bumper of a moving car to be pulled along, you're hooky bobbing. You've hooked yourself to the car or truck, and you'll bob along. The best thing to say about hooky bobbing is: don't do it. Hooking on to a moving vehicle is dangerous. So tell all those kids in Idaho, "Don't even think of hooky bobbing here."

Jack ditch. The way to order a Jack Daniel's with water in Montana. The "ditch" means water.

jackalope. An unusual creature that somehow got by Darwin, the jackalope is a rabbit with antler ears—part jackrabbit, part antelope. It's found primarily in Wyoming and particularly in Douglas, Wyoming, which was originally named Antelope and is now the Jackalope Capital of the Nation. Two taxidermists, Douglas and Ralph Herrick, discovered the jackalope in the 1930s— or rather, discovered how easy it was to dupe clueless city slickers into believing there was such a creature. Yes, jackalope is a joke, but that bit about Douglas once being Antelope is true. The town was renamed after Stephen Douglas.

jockey box. Sometimes you find testaments to days gone by in the oddest places . . . like the glove compartment of a car. Jockey box is what some folks in Utah, Wyoming, Idaho, and other parts of the Northwest call a glove compartment. The term is a vestige of those wagon train days when people were moving west. The box beneath the seat of the driver—who drove horses rather than cars—was called the jockey box.

lamb licker. What a sheepherder's likely to be called in Montana, since at least the 1930s.

live dictionary. Cowboy-ese for a schoolteacher, most of whom were female at the time of coining. No doubt the schoolteacher could find many terms in her dictionary to use in reply.

long butt. Forget any visions of anatomy that may be popping into the brain. This long butt is the defective part of a tree that the loggers have cut off. The term has a long history: it's more than a century old.

the mountain is out today. What Seattleites say on days they can see Mount Rainier. (Fittingly for Seattle's drizzly weather, "Rainier" is spelled as if to say "more rainy"—that is, rain-ier—but it's pronounced "ruh-neer.") If the mountain is out, chances are the sun is, too. You're most likely to hear the expression from the newer residents of this oft-overcast city. Old-timers are used to the mountain going in and out of the mist. *Not so fast*, say Portlanders. They've been known to say the same thing about Oregon's Mount Hood in their equally misty city. Oregon weather forecasters will sometimes announce a **sunbreak**, a rare occurrence in parts of the state.

no-host bar. What's known elsewhere as a cash bar. "No-host" first appeared in 1967, in Washington State. Party throwers in Oregon, Idaho, and Montana also picked up the expression. It has since migrated south to California, where the *Los Angeles Times* used it in a headline in 1998. A **no-host dinner** is another way to say Dutch treat: we each pay for our own.

ooferfun. How a Utah native is apt to pronounce "oh for fun." The way many other Americans would say, for example, "oh, how exciting" becomes "oh, for exciting" in Utah-ese. The construction was first recorded in 1988 but was probably on locals' tongues long before then.

oose. If you Google "oose," you're likely to get information on object-oriented software engineering. But if you ask a Utahn, you just might hear that it's what the yucca plant has been called in these parts since at least the 1860s.

piggle. To pull on nervously. This nervous tic seems to be one that only people in parts of Wyoming exhibit— at least by this name. Dig down into the language a bit and you'll find that the term was used in the 1880s by the English miners who came to Wyoming.

potlatch. If someone in the Pacific Northwest or Alaska invites you to a potlatch, don't mistake this for **potluck**, or what used to be called in Indiana **pitch-in dinner**. Because you're in luck: you don't have to bring any kind of **covered dish** (North Dakota, Minnesota) or **casserole** (Illinois) or **carry-in** (Ohio) or **scramble dinner** (Illinois again) to this gathering. Potlatch, the Chinook for *p'achitl*, is the Native American name for a feast where the host gives the guests some really good loot. The more important the guest, the better the gifts. Try to score an invite.

Rocky Mountain oysters. Okay, so you know oysters can't really live in mountains, right? That means this must be a euphemism for—that's right: steer testicles. "Fry 'em up and they're great," assures one Colorado aficionado. If they look like oysters, does that mean they taste like chicken?

silver thaw. Freezing rain. But shouldn't a thaw melt rather than freeze, you ask? Look, they've been calling them silver thaws in the Pacific Northwest since at least 1936, when somebody actually wrote it down. They also say it clear across the continent, in Newfoundland. Just remember, if somebody says silver thaw, an ice storm is coming.

skookum. Powerful, brave, good, strong, the best. This all-purpose Chinook word for all kinds of superlatives has been in the Alaskan and Northwest lexicons since the mid-1800s at least. But skookum can also spook 'em: another meaning is ghost, evil spirit, monster. Context is everything.

ride the SLUT. The public transportation system that was installed in one of Seattle's neighborhoods is supposed to be called the South Lake Union Streetcar. That may be its official name, but a streetcar is a trolley, and so that *t* makes the system a SLUT. Memo to bureaucrats: always test the names you're thinking about giving a project for an unfortunate acronym. SLUT gives new meaning to *A Streetcar Named Desire*.

sockeye salmon. In Alaska and the Pacific Northwest, they don't bat an eye at this term. It's the American attempt to say and spell *suk-keya*, a word in the native Salish language that means "redfish." Can you guess what color these salmon are? (It's because of the krill they eat.) The Sac Foodies, a band of PR pros in Sacramento with a taste for good food, say they learned from an Alaska tour guide to count off the five kinds of salmon in the region like so: "thumb for chum; forefinger for sockeye (like sticking a finger in the eye); middle finger is king; ring finger is silver; and pinkie, of course, for pink."

The Coffee Brewhaha

"They have in Turky a drink called coffee," wrote Sir Francis Bacon (1561–1626) rather wistfully, "made of a berry of the same name, as black as soot, and of a strong scent, but not aromatical; which they take, beaten into powder, in water, as hot as they can drink it. This drink comforteth the brain and heart, and helpeth digestion."

Captain John Smith is credited with bringing the drink that comforteth to the colonies, to Virginia in 1607. It didn't take long for coffee to replace beer as the breakfast drink of choice in New York City. Coffee caught on even more during the time leading up to the Revolutionary War, when Americans were boycotting tea as part of their famous protest against the British. It became patriotic to drink coffee. But it was also pricey, so Americans often found themselves resorting to coffee made of barley or rye, aka **Boston coffee**. In the mid-1800s there was even a version called **crumb coffee**, made with burned bread crumbs. Yum. But once coffee became cheap commercially, it became ubiquitous.

Beginning in the 1850s, we called coffee **java**, the name of the Indonesian island where much of it was grown. **Mocha** also became a generic term for coffee. It wasn't long before we figured out that coffee was a delicious accompaniment to crumbs—provided they weren't burned bread crumbs, but rather, a nice pastry. Combine that with some good conversation (some would call it gossip), and the German **kaffee-klatsch** was a staple of many an American home.

Maxwell House coffee, though a brand name, was initially tied to a place: the Maxwell House hotel in Nashville, Tennessee. Theodore Roosevelt is credited with giving the coffee the slogan "good to the last drop." Meanwhile, farther west, the cowboys were asking for a cup of **Arbuckles**, a brand so popular in the West that the name became synonymous with coffee. **Black water** and **brown gargle** were also cowboy-speak, no doubt for coffee that was, as the saying went, **strong enough to float a colt**.

Before the days of fancy lattes and cappuccinos, a **cuppa joe** was a commonly heard reference to coffee. Some say the phrase dates back to 1914, when the U.S. Secretary of the Navy, Josephus Daniels, banned wine in the officers' mess. He recommended coffee instead. But others admonish those who would swallow this story to wake up and smell the coffee. "A cuppa joe" is tied to the military—that part is true—but simply refers to the idea of coffee being the drink for the average Joe. (This was pre-Starbucks, remember.)

Okay, so let's go with the regular-Joe story. The truly burning question among today's coffee drinkers is: just what is a "regular" coffee?

That's easy, say those in the West and most other parts of the country: it's black.

No way, say East Coasters. "Regular" means with milk and sugar in many parts of the Northeast—what some in Chicago would (again) call Boston coffee. Java junkies in New Orleans also expect cream and sugar when they order their coffee regular. Alternatively, you can ask for it **light and sweet**.

Just to confuse matters, in Rhode Island you can drink **coffee milk**. It's not coffee with milk, though—it's milk with coffee syrup.

Anyone for hot chocolate?

spendy. New Englanders may be known for minding their pennies, but it's Northwesterners who have the word for things that cost too much: spendy, as in too expensive. People who understand spendy are often thrifty and not likely to be spendthrifts.

Tacoma aroma. The name coined in the 1930s for the smell this Washington city used to constantly exude because of the area's paper mills. The sulfur emissions have been significantly reduced since then, so Tacoma has less aroma.

3-7-77. Montana's magic numbers . . . depending on which side of the law you're on. In the days when Montana was still a territory, the vigilante enforcers of justice would summon the numbers 3-7-77 when they wanted to drop a hint as to what might happen if you made trouble. These were not numbers to gamble with. They signified the size of the grave they'd be digging for you if you broke the law: 3 feet wide, 7 feet long, 77 inches deep. Note to those planning a run-in with the law here: today the decal of the Montana Highway Patrol features the numbers 3-7-77.

HOT DIGGETY!

Rhode Island has its improbably named NEW YORK SYSTEM and Maryland its FRIZZLED, but other places in the country can claim they're top (hot) dog, too. Can you guess where you're most likely to find these hot dogs?

1. Half-smoke
2. Sonoran
3. Red Hot
4. Coney
5. Dixie
6. Ripper

ANSWERS

1. Washington, DC, is home of the half-smoke, a hot dog that can actually be lightly smoked or simply split in half.

2. In Tucson, Arizona, the Sonoran comes wrapped in bacon; topped with pinto beans, tomatoes, and onions; and garnished with hot sauce.

3. Chicago, land of the big winter chill, serves a hot dog laden with peppers, onions, relish, and tomatoes. A poppy seed roll is often what holds the Red Hot together. Red Hot is the name of both the dog and the company, Red Hot Chicago, that's made them famous.

4. Michigan and Oklahoma are among the outposts for the hot dog named after Coney Island in New York. (Is it any wonder our kids are geographically challenged?) Chili is the mainstay of the Coney, with onions and pickle mustard frequent accompaniments.

5. West Virginia has the distinction of serving the first Dixie dog, back in the 1930s. It's where cole slaw meets meat sauce meets hot dog.

6. In hot dog havens throughout New Jersey, they deep-fry the sausage till the skin splits open—the better for the Ripper to welcome the onions and peppers.

up to Green River. When you do something full bore, no-holds-barred, you're doing it to the hilt. In Old West parlance, that's up to Green River, this being the name of a manufacturer of knives. When you shoved one of those knives in to the hilt, that's where the name "Green River" was stamped.

WE'RE IN THE TOOLIES

Alaska

Think Pacific Northwest at subzero and that's part of what goes into Alaska-speak. So does the language of the native Alaskans and the legacy of the gold prospectors.

arctic wine. The Alaskan euphemism for whiskey, straight up and smooth going down. The term was first recorded in 1939 but odds are the locals had been enjoying their arctic wine long before then. Do not serve this vintage chilled.

banana belt. The warm regions of a cold place. Until Alaska became a state in 1959, the only place in the nation you were likely to hear this was in South Dakota. The expression predates that of global warming . . . or perhaps prefigures it. Now a number of cold places with relatively hot spots claim banana belts for themselves. But for sheer oddity of juxtaposition, the forty-ninth state gets first claim.

bingle. Relatively worthless money. The term for this coinage was coined around 1921. At the time a bingle was worth about ten cents (even back then, nobody really cared if all you could spare was a dime). The federal government minted bingles and used them in connection with an agricultural project in the state. They got to be worth as much as ten dollars.

Cheechako. Look what the Chinook wind blew in—a Johnny-come-lately, Alaska/Northwest style. Cheechako is Chinook for one who comes lately: a newcomer. In the 1890s, the tenderfoots trying to work the mines earned this sobriquet. Chinook is the language of Native Americans populating parts of Washington and Oregon from way back; they were anything but Cheechakos. Today "Chinook" often refers to the warm wind that blows onto this part of the coast.

iron dog. Snowmobile in Alaska. It has long been the custom in this country to pair "iron" with the animal that originally did the work that the newfangled conveyance now does. Thus trains used to be referred to as the "iron horse." In this case, the snowmobile is doing the work that sled dogs traditionally did. The Iron Dog is now also the name for its own style of Iditarod. Begun in 1984, it's billed as the world's longest snowmobile race—nearly two thousand miles. Mush!

outside. You'd think that in a great-outdoors place like Alaska, "outside" would mean "outdoors." It doesn't. "Outside" is anywhere but Alaska to an Alaskan, and has been since at least 1896, the first recorded reference to outside. From the Alaskan perspective, the whole rest of the country it's a part of is outside.

Sitka slippers. These go by another name, too: **Alaskan tennis shoes**. Actually, they're neither slipper nor shoe, but rather heavy-duty knee-high rubber boots to wear in bad weather.

sourdough. An old-timer in Alaska, and no doubt many of these old-timers could tell you how they got that name. It started when the Klondike miners headed north to the future, in the early 1900s. It's not like there were bakeries in Alaska. So the miners brought their own dough "starter"—the mix of flour and water—for leavening bread. This was the start of sourdough bread. Sourdough didn't need the kind of yeast other breads did, so it was better suited to a cold, isolated place that wasn't known for its grocery stores. And yes, the dough did smell sour—but the bread tasted delicious.

If the Shoe Skulks . . .

If you were to ask for a pair of sneakers in the eighteenth century, you were likely to get two large drinking vessels—figure about five gallons per—and a curious stare. But by the 1870s, you'd get something to wear on your feet. They might even be called tennis shoes, as they were in an 1887 volume of the *Boston Journal of Education*.

The idea behind the name "sneaker" was that it was a stealth shoe: its silent rubber sole made it possible to skulk around and sneak up on someone. Why that would be so desirable is a puzzle, unless you were a gumshoe. "Gumshoe" is just a vowel away from "gym shoe," the gum indicating rubber, as in the sneaky soles. "Gumshoe" became slang for detective, one who is given to skulking around.

The rubber-soled shoes, meanwhile, became popular with basketball players. Even though you can hear the squeak-squeak-squeak of the shoes as the players make their way around today's arenas, they've stayed sneakers and not squeakers.

"Athletic shoe" is a more generic term for this footwear, but Americans don't much take to generic names—too vanilla. **Tennis shoes** are what you're likely to wear in much of the Midwest, including North Dakota, Kansas, Ohio, and parts of Illinois. In Chicago, though, they're **gym shoes**. Kansas City, Missouri, is definitely the land of tennis shoes. Californians' first choice is tennis shoes—in parts of Southern California, including San Diego, you might hear **tennies**—but they'll also settle for **sneakers**. In Maryland, you're likely to hear either. Long Islanders and Rhode Islanders emphatically wear sneakers. That's what they wear in the Mid-Atlantic states, too. In New Jersey, sometimes they're just **sneaks** (the shoes, not the people). Floridians favor sneakers, while Puerto Ricans take to tennis shoes. But in Nashville, Tennessee, they have everyone beat. They don't wear any of these; they wear **skips**.

Thankfully, Americans have put enough of their British past behind them not to call these shoes what the Brits do—"pumps" for some mysterious reason (get the gumshoe on it), or "trainers," which conjures up images of training wheels.

These days, the name of the manufacturer—make that the brand—often supplants regional terms, especially if you're swooshing around in a pair of Nike athletic shoes. Converse was the first to put some rubber into that game, with its 1917 Converse All Star basketball shoe. And baby boomers may well recall that whether they wore sneakers, tennis shoes, or gym shoes as kids, what they really had on their feet were Keds.

Spenard divorce. A quickie divorce, Anchorage style. It's named after a section of the city with lots of bars and marital discord. In a Spenard divorce, there's often another man or woman in the picture. Oh, and did we mention: guns as well.

stack robber. A gizmo that's a kind of Robin Hood of heating. You attach this metal box to your stovepipe and it disperses more heat into the room than up the chimney. The one being robbed is the heating company.

sundog. When it's very cold in Alaska and very bright, a circle of color appears to surround the sun. That's a sundog. Sundogs get around, though. Thousands of miles away on the tiny island of Smith Island, off the Maryland coast, people have been known to call this phenomenon by the same name.

in the toolies. It seems odd to those of us OUTSIDE to think that a state we associate with wilderness would have its own word for such, but there you are. Toolies are the boonies. The expression was first recorded in the 1960s, and it's one that Alaskans might possibly have borrowed from their Canadian neighbors, who know a thing or two about middle-of-nowhere. It's quite possibly a cousin to *tule*, the Spanish word that Californians appropriated for their marshlands back in the 1800s.

"Time to Make the Olykoeks"

The Pilgrims had a long layover in Holland before finally setting sail for America. Like anyone else stuck in a place, they ate—doughnuts, among other things, a sweet Dutch pastry of deep-fried dough. Puritanism be damned, the Pilgrims liked the tempting confection, and eventually it became part of America's breakfast as well as an apparently essential nutrient for police officers.

Olykoek was the unappetizing name for this deep-fried dough: "oily cake" in Dutch. Fortunately, Washington Irving came along in 1809 and gave the sweet fried dough the more inviting name of dough nut. The dough was formed in a solid ball that resembled a nut.

So there you had the doughnut—but not the hole. In fact, a number of variations of this sweet fried dough are still holeless.

The **beignet** is a New Orleans version of a doughnut, minus the hole and in a rectangular shape. The **doughboy** is a New England version and has the same powdered-sugar coating as the beignet, but is rounder. In the Southwest, a doughboy is a **buñuelo**.

The term "doughboy" was recorded as early as 1752 in Boston and described as "a dumpling" that could be made with cornmeal. One theory for why soldiers were called doughboys has it that the big brass buttons on their uniforms resembled the dumpling shape of the edible version of the doughboy.

Thank the Pennsylvania Dutch for the hole in the doughnut putting. It's how they made their **fasnacht**, the holey doughnut they ate on Shrove Tuesday—aka Fat Tuesday, the last day before Lent to indulge in sweet temptations. That's probably why, in the Amish region of Pennsylvania, doughnuts are **fat cakes**.

The Pennsylvania Dutch also put the *dunken* into doughnuts, starting the custom of dipping these **dunkers**. The other Dutch—the ones from Holland—sometimes called their doughnuts **crullers** if they had a curly shape. You still hear this term in parts of the Mid-Atlantic.

New England boasts a number of old terms for doughnuts. **Boil cakes** is one, and pretty boring. Try, instead, **cymbals**, as the doughnuts took on this shape. Or **huffjuff** or **huffle juffle**. The term means "to swell," the way deep-fried dough does.

Then there are the holey-er-than-thou terms: **holy pokes** in Connecticut, **Baptist bread** (or **Baptist cake**) in Maine. Why Baptist? Because the dough is immersed.

In the Great Lakes region, doughnuts are **fried cakes**, a term that dates back to the 1830s. Wisconsin has a jelly or custard variety known as the **Berliner**, first cousin to the often oblong **bismarck** (aka **long john**) in the upper Midwest. Michiganites sometimes munch on a **lunch roll**, which is comparable.

Bear sign is cowboy-ese for doughnut, the term dating back to the early 1900s in New Mexico. Salt

Lake City invented a version in 1939 called the **spud-nut**, borrowing potatoes from Idaho to make the flour.

So much for "doughnut." Now for the pressing question: who took the "ugh" out of "doughnut" and made it "donut"? Your theories, hypotheses, and tall tales welcome.

Calendar note: June 5 is National Donut Day. Celebrate with your favorite olykoek. (Ugh.)

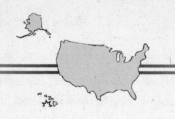

WIKI WIKI

Hawaii

Just about every group that's found its way to these islands has left something of its language.

The true Hawaiian language is Polynesian, but a pidgin English was cooked up when England's Captain James Cook came to the islands in the 1770s. Then came the New England missionaries in the early 1800s, hell-bent on converting the natives to English. Later on came the waves of other immigrants—from China and Japan, Portugal and Spain, Korea and the Philippines. As a result, the Hawaiian vocabulary has lots of loanwords—those adopted from other languages but made their own. Hawaii-speak is as colorful and curious as its flora and fauna.

ahahana. "Shame on you," Hawaiian style, especially when you're scolding children. It's one of those loan-words that haoles, or non-Hawaiians, might consider borrowing for its melodious quality.

bumbeye. This term, meaning "soon" or "some other time," is not far from the English "by and by." It was actually heard in New England in 1722 and in the South about a century later, among the slaves. By and by, bumbeye found its way from the cotton plantations of the South to the sugar plantations of Hawaii. One account says that missionaries brought the term to Hawaii in the hymn "In the Sweet By-and-By," composed in 1868.

bumboocha. Gigunda in Hawaiian—something really, really big.

calabash cousin. The beloved soul you call aunt or uncle or grandma, even though she or he isn't one, relatively speaking. But the two of you are so close, you "eat from the same calabash." Literally, you eat from the same hollowed-out gourd. So close, in other words, it's as if you're related.

da kine. If you want to sound like a native (good luck), embrace this term. Literally, it means "these kinds," but it's become a chameleon phrase that takes on various meaning depending on context. Often "da kine" is code for "it's all good."

Dole's beard. Hawaii's version of Spanish moss. It's named after Sanford Dole. Nothing to do with pineapples—this gentleman was the first president of the Republic of Hawaii in the 1890s, and later its governor. His long, flowing gray beard was practically iconic.

holoholo. A good time, Hawaiian style.

hoomalimali. Schmoozy-woozy, aloha style. In other words, flattery. It does double duty as a verb, to flatter.

kama'aina. A native Hawaiian, as opposed to a haole or MALIHINI. Ironically, the term was first recorded by just such a foreigner in 1826. Literally translated, it means "child of the land." Today it also connotes well established. Many long-standing businesses will use this in their names.

Porch, Piazza, or Lanai?

What do you call the place that connects the outside of your house to the inside, and that's known for inviting swings and rockers? In much of the country, it's a porch, from Latin *porticus*, which became the English *portico*. In parts of the Northeast and Midwest, though, wherever the Dutch decided to set a spell, that porch is a **stoop**. The Dutch *stoep* means "front verandah."

Verandah is the long, languorous word that's long been attached to the South. The word is rooted in Hindi, and if it's one thing the southern United States and much of India have in common, it's heat. The verandah was where you fled out to in the days before you fled into air-conditioning, to escape the heat and the sun. On really hot nights, you even slept out on the **sleeping porch**, although this porch might be more enclosed than the generally open verandah.

In parts of the South such as Mississippi, the porch is a **gallery**. In Florida you'll always find a porch on a Florida **cracker house**. A cracker house, such as the type that Marjorie Kinnan Rawlings lived in when she moved to central Florida, has a wide overhang above the front porch that keeps not only the sun off but the torrential summer rains as well.

"Cracker" is the name sometimes given to old-time Floridians (and Georgians) who live in rural areas. It's an old, Elizabethan-era word (Shakespeare used it in *King John*) connected to the idea of conversation. The fact that "cracker" is connected to both conversation and the concept of a front porch brings up a main point about parking yourself on whatever you may call this spot.

Before there was social media, there was the front porch, the place where you greeted your neighbors who were passing by and you sat and talked about the day's news. Okay, you gossiped. It was how the writer Russell Baker learned a whole lot about his family when he was a little kid, listening to the grown-ups on the front porch. In recent years there's been a resurgence of this front-porch friendliness among the architects of the New Urbanism. Go to places like Kentlands, Maryland, and Seaside, Florida, and in these new communities you'll see lots of old-fashioned porches.

In Hawaii, a porch is called a **lanai**. New Englanders, especially those along the coast, have **decks**, raised roofless porches that are usually in the back of the house but occasionally wrap around to the front. But in certain parts of New England, including the Boston area, a porch is often a **piazza**. In Italian, that's a town square, a place to gather—which is exactly what people do on the porch.

lolo. Just one letter away from the Spanish *loco*, which is what lolo means. Okay, "stupid" or "crazy," if you want to be mean about it. It's another one of those loan-words, and at least one person on the island was considered a little goofy in 1938, because it was recorded back then. Lolo literally means paralyzed. Remember: if you go HOLOHOLO you just might get a little lolo-lolo.

maikai. Good, well, or goodness—take your pick. Use this all-purpose feel-good word as an adjective, adverb, or noun. Careful on the spelling—if you miss that first *i*, you'll go in a totally different direction linguistically. See the next entry . . .

makai and **mauka.** Makai means toward the sea, mauka means toward the mountains. Those are pretty much the only two ways you can go on these volcanic islands. The terms—Hawaii's own type of GPS—were recorded as early as 1873. So forget east and west. Act like a KAMA'AINA and adopt the Hawaiian compass.

malihini. A tourist (and therefore a stranger); a new-comer (and therefore a novice). A close cousin in terms of estrangement is **haole**, or foreigner—more specifically, Caucasians. "To the natives, all whites are haoles—*how-ries*—that is, strangers, or, more properly, foreigners," wrote Mark Twain in 1866.

Any Way You Stack 'Em . . .

"Pancake," pronounced Noah Webster in his 1806 *Compendious Dictionary of the English Language*: "a kind of thin cake fried in a pan."

This man of many defined words was nothing if not cryptic. "Pan" might seem straightforward enough—the thing you cook the thin cake in. But some say this "pan" is not a derivative of the Latin *patina*, or vessel, but is instead from the Latin *panem*, meaning bread. Take away the *i* from the French for bread—*pain*—and you have, once again, "pan." Hence a pantry is a place to store bread, not pans.

Consider how ubiquitous a pancake is in one form or another worldwide, let alone nationwide, and the suggestion of "bread," in its sense of common sustenance, gains currency. In fact, a pancake may be the world's oldest type of bread. In Mexico it's called a tortilla; in Russia, a blintz; in France, a crêpe, and like many French, it's *très* thin. The English way back when made a boozy version out of ale.

Today the Brits might top theirs with powdered sugar and the Germans adorn theirs with jam. To North Americans belongs the maple syrup. And everybody but us seems to use this versatile cake as a roll-up, filling it with either sweets or savories. The closest Americans come is the occasional pigs-in-a-blanket, sausages that are wrapped sometimes in pancakes but other times in dough.

Some of the first American settlers would have called their pancakes **buckwheat cakes**, thanks to the Dutch, who brought this first wheat pancake with them in the early eighteenth century.

By the end of that century Americans were making them out of both wheat and cornmeal and calling them **slapjacks**: the cook would slap them onto a skillet. Slapjack is just one letter away from **flapjack**, suggesting that the cake was flipped over in the skillet. New England author Nathaniel Hawthorne (1804–64) used both terms.

"Jack" is no guy in particular, just a jack-of-all-trades name that worked well. Flapjack is actually a word from Elizabethan English, and it's the Ozarks and Appalachia that have done a good job of preserving it.

Hotcake is another old-time term for pancake, probably an American way to say the Dutch *heetekoek*. We must have been eating a lot of them by the early nineteenth century because we were already equating popularity with the idea of "selling like hotcakes." The expression was one of the few things the North and South could agree on during the Civil War.

Pele's hair, or **Pele's whiskers.** The name Hawaiians started giving volcanic glass as early as at least the 1840s. Pele is the Hawaiian goddess of all things fiery, including volcanoes.

Pele's tear. Take a droplet of volcanic glass from the end of Pele's hair: that's one of Pele's tears.

wiki wiki. Not what you may think, all you Wikipediacs. Listen to its cadence—sounds a bit like "hurry, hurry," doesn't it? That's because it means quickly or fast. But there is, indeed, a connection between the Hawaiian wiki wiki and web-based wikis: the programmer who developed the software that made it easier to edit information quickly on collaborative sites named it "wiki" after the Hawaiian word.

BREAKFAST QUIZ

Can you guess which part of the country you're having breakfast in by the name for pancakes?

1. **GRIDDLE CAKE:** New England or the South?
2. **BATTER:** Mississippi, South Carolina, or Louisiana?
3. **FLITTER CAKE:** Southwest or Southern Gulf?
4. **FLANNEL CAKE:** Pacific Northwest or Midwest?

5. **JOE FLOGGER:** Ozarks, Appalachia, or New England coast?

ANSWERS:

GRIDDLE CAKE is a Southernism for pancake, as is **BATTERCAKE**—or sometimes, in South Carolina, just **BATTER. FLITTER CAKE** is what's served in the Southern Gulf area. To flitter is to flutter, or move quickly, and when making pancakes, it's best to be fast when you flip. In Arkansas, they take this to the extreme, sometimes calling their pancakes **JUMPOVERS.** The cowboys were more slapdash in their approach and used sourdough to make their **SPLATTERDABS.**

In parts of the Midwest, you're eating **FLANNEL CAKES.** This has nothing to do with the soft fabric; "flannen" is a Scots-Irish term for oatcake.

A Jewish cook might opt for **LATKES,** potato pancakes.

In a few places along the New England coast, you might still be able to get pancakes and not just a strange look if you ask for a **JOE FLOGGER.** Head to the Northwest and you might find **ENGLISH SADDLES** in Idaho, **HORSE BLANKETS** in Oregon, and **SADDLE BLANKETS** or even **MONKEY BLANKETS** in Washington.

STACK CAKES is another name, and one that makes perfect sense. Pancakes, after all, are often served in a stack. But how curious that, although we describe something as being "flat as a pancake," we've never called our pancakes "flatcakes."

CRACKING TEETH

The Nearly Lost Lexicons of America

In small pockets of America—north, south, east, west—can still be heard the vestiges of near-forgotten dialects and expressions. Before they disappear and we lose these linguistic delights, here is a sampling of their sayings.

Appalachia and the Ozarks

Thank their mountain ranges, a natural barrier, for keeping some of the distinctive expressions of Appalachia and the Ozarks separate from the surrounding areas. Both were once very isolated, rural regions, and they still have traces of this remoteness. Appalachia, which boasts the Blue Ridge and Smoky Mountains, cuts a swath through thirteen states. It encompasses all of West Virginia and portions of Mississippi, Alabama, Georgia, Tennessee, South Carolina, North Carolina, Kentucky, Virginia, Ohio, Pennsylvania, Maryland, and New York. The Scots-Irish who settled here in the 1700s helped set the linguistic tone, but so have the blacks and Native Americans in the region.

The Ozark Mountains are what join Arkansas and Missouri in common linguistic ground, along with parts of Oklahoma and Kansas. Some of the people of the Ozarks are descended from those in Appalachia.

arkansaw. It may appear to be a more phonetic pronunciation of Arkansas, but in the Ozarks, it means to cheat someone or take advantage of them. The expression was recorded as early as the 1920s.

barking spiders. Farts in the Ozarks, although it's doubtful anybody can tell you why. Let's face it—have you ever heard a spider pass gas? Perhaps the arachnid in Australia that goes by this name does so. But this bark seems to have a certain bite: in parts of northern Florida, gassy passings have been heard to be called **barking frogs**. Best to give wide berth to someone announcing the barking of anything but a dog.

black-actually. There's true, and then there's absolutely, positively, certifiably true. That's black-actually in the Ozarks, and it's black-actually true that people here have been heard saying this since the late 1920s at least. Occasionally it comes out as back-actually.

boomer. This boomer has nothing to do with a genera-tion. Rather, it's a red squirrel, and it's been called that in print since 1878. It's a great gotcha word to try on your friends.

bush up. How people in the Ozarks hide—particularly when they're finding cover in the bushes.

check. If in Appalachia someone asks if you'll take a check, don't expect to get money. Do get ready to have a snack or a light meal. Last time we checked, there was a record of "check" being used in Appalachia as far back as the American Revolution.

it's clabbering up. That means it's clouding over, an expression first recorded in the 1930s. *Clabber* is from the Gaelic *clabair*, a cousin of "churn." Clabber milk, which is curdled, used to be common in parts of the United States, including the South. It was thick and formed curds; thus thick, lumpy-looking clouds resembled clabber. You come across the word when you buy Clabber Girl cornstarch, which is a thickener. Cottage cheese is sometimes called clabber cheese (when it's not being called SMEARCASE). *Bainne clabair*, or clabbered milk, is sometimes heard as **bonnyclapper** in portions of the Midwest and as **clobber** in parts of the South.

that dog won't hunt. Folks in the Ozarks were among the first to say "that won't work" by saying "that dog won't hunt." That dog's not been hunting since at least the 1930s. It's also been roaming, as the expression has tracked its way across a wide swath of the South. A kissing-cousin phrase is **that cock won't fight**. Happily, sometimes something does work, in which case, "that dog'll hunt."

don't let the door hit you where the Lord split you. In other words, don't be slow to leave—especially because you've just ticked off the person who's flinging this phrase at you. The hope is that the door that's slamming on you will close fast enough to whack you on the butt.

fraidy hole. It's where scaredy-cats go during tornadoes, and aren't they the smarty-pants for doing so. Cyclone cellars have been called fraidy-holes since at least 1914.

Georgia ice cream. What people in the Ozarks and northern Florida fondly call grits. Grits are a dish of ground corn that Southerners eat with many meals. The word harks back to Old English—even though no English, old or otherwise, have a clue about grits except those who've visited the American South (and even then they wonder). "Grits" is from *grytta*, meaning "groats," or coarse meal. Northerners don't really know what to make of grits. They sometimes try to make them a cereal with milk and sugar, which causes Southerners to grit their teeth.

larrupin. Extremely. Just like WICKED, "larrupin" is joined at the hip with "good." The proper spelling is "larruping," but nobody bothers with that *g* when saying something was larrupin good. And lots of people say it. You'll hear it not just in this part of the country but in Texas and Oklahoma as well. Back in the 1920s, it was a common expression in California, and it's still popular in the West. *Larrup* is its root, and that has to do with thrashing or whipping. Hey, the Brits have their "smashing" for meaning excellent; we can have our "thrashing" derivative for meaning extremely good.

mother wit. Common sense. See? Mom really does know best. "Mother wit" means the kind of smarts you don't get from book learning but rather from heeding the collective wisdom that's passed down. It's another of the terms once heard in New England, as recorded in 1858, but now more at home in points south.

poke. This poke is a pouch, or, as Webster's *Compendious Dictionary* of 1806 defined it, "a small bag." "Poke" dates back to the fourteenth century, and it started out as the Celtic *poc* (think "pocket"). Ever heard the expression "a pig in a poke"? It means something worthless that you were conned into buying. The first such sucker, way back when at an English country fair, thought he was buying a piglet in a sack, only to find out when he opened the sack that there was no pig in the poke; it was a cat instead.

rush the growler. Abandon all linguistic logic if you're trying to deduce what this might mean. Nothing is growling and nobody's rushing. It means to fill a lunch bucket with beer. The expression first surfaced in the late 1800s, in New York City, in an article in the *New York Herald*. Then it headed north and west, but also to the coal country of Pennsylvania. The metal pail that held a miner's meal for midday—the growler—would be filled up again on the way home—rushed—with beer from the local bar.

sad cake. An old-fashioned dense cake that tends to sink in the middle. That's not why it's sad, though. Sad, way back when, meant *sated*—that is, full. Sad cakes are a vestige of old coal-mining days. They originated in the coal and mill country of Lancashire in northern England, and then made their way across the Pond to the southern United States.

si-gogglin. Anything but straight—that is, off center, at an angle, askew, crooked, crosswise. It was recorded as "si-godlin" in 1896, the "si" a shortcut for "side." It's a sideways-sounding word, and "sideways" is close to its meaning.

tighter than Dick's hatband. Something as odd as can be. Bartlett's *Dictionary of Americanisms* takes the expression back to 1848, a time when "Dick's hatband" was at varying intervals a way to say cursed, contrary, crooked, or queer. No one has quite figured out who Dick was, but look for someone with a too-large head and a too-small hat. Silas House, the author of *Clay's Quilt*, says this expression is one he often hears in his Appalachia home.

The Bankers and the O'cockers

In the early 1700s, people from the Tidewater area of Virginia and the eastern shore of Maryland struck out for someplace new and ended up on the Outer Banks of North Carolina, including the island of Ocracoke. Thus they became the Bankers and the O'cockers, and certain aspects of their linguistic heritage of south-western England mixed with Scots-Irish to become their own vernacular.

begombed. If it's begombed it's begrimed: it's dirty.

dingbatter. Dingbatter isn't from this area originally, but it may be a word you hear frequently on Ocracoke Island because most of us are dingbatters—outsiders to the island. Don't look for lofty etymology here. It's actually an Archie Bunkerism, from the 1970s television sitcom *All in the Family*. Archie would often refer to his wife, Edith, as a dingbat.

fetch up. How islanders show up. "Fetch up" elsewhere means to reach a goal.

goodsome. The O'cocker answer to WICKED. If it's ex-ceptionally good, it's goodsome. The opposite is also true: if it's awful, it's **badsome**. Just don't say "it's a goodsome thing." When you use these "somes," they have to be the last word in the phrase.

mommucked. Badgered. The word is a ghost of the Elizabethan English past that is part of the island's linguistic legacy. Shakespeare used the word, but his mommuck meant to tear to shreds. Time and the ever-evolving English language stand still for no man, not even Big Will.

I'm quamished in the gut. You're sick to your stomach. Quamished is an old word recorded back in 1787. Most of us would say we don't use it, but in one sense we do, whenever we call upon "qualm."

she sure can say a word. Meaning, she sure can say many words; she sure is talkative.

let's go for a scud. If an islander invites you for a scud, chances are you're going for a car ride. The word started off as a seafaring term; it has to do with how a boat handles in a gale. This surf term has become a turf term here.

Bonac

Go to the Hamptons in Long Island and you're likely to find outsized homes and outsized prices for arugula. But long before eastern Long Island became the bastion of the hyperrich, it was home to a group of fishing families known as the Bonackers, whose ancestors settled here in the 1600s. Today you have to look hard and listen harder, but you might actually find the last gasps of their way of life and manner of speaking. It clings as tenaciously to a life of the sea as barnacles to a boat.

Bonacker—or Bonacer, or Bonac—is from *Accabonac*, a word rooted in the Native American language of the area. **Bubs**, or **bubbies**, as Bonackers call themselves, don't necessarily **say something** (talk a lot). But when they do, they have some interesting ways of saying things.

clean the tide out. Be the last to leave (a party, usually).

Long Island hurry. This means nothing like a New York minute. It's a kind of potato stew.

Sputnik grass. A spongy, tubular seaweed first spotted around the time the Russians sent Sputnik into space, in 1957.

up the island. In the direction of New York City. (See DOWN THE CAPE for how this geography works.)

upstreeters. Going upstreet used to mean heading toward the commercial part of town. Now "upstreeters" refers to the wealthy, mainly summer enclave that's made the Hamptons ultra-upscale.

wouldn't get inside ten clam rakes of it. Wouldn't touch it with a ten-foot pole.

Boontling

Long before Valley Girl days, a tiny vest pocket of Northern California had its own way of speaking. Unlike most things California, Boontling jargon never went beyond where it was born: in Boonville, a small town in Mendocino County's Anderson Valley. Boontling ("Boon" + "lingo") had its heyday in the late 1800s and early 1900s. Most likely it came about as a way for some of the locals to distance themselves from strangers. Very few people speak it now, but some younger residents are keeping it on life support.

One of the charms of Boontling is its penchant for naming objects after some of the locals. Try it with your own name: if you were an object or a character trait, what would you be? Now you're **harping boont** (speaking Boontling).

Bill Nunn. Syrup, because Bill Nunn poured it prodigiously on his food.

Charlie. To embarrass, because it didn't take much to do just that to Charlie Ball.

Frati. Wine, after the local vintner.

Walter. The phone, named after the first person in Boonville to have one, Walter Levi.

Zeese. Coffee, after Zacharia Clifton Blevens, or Z. C. for short. Say it fast and it sounds like "zeese." The man loved his coffee. Tip: ask for a **horn of Zeese** if you want to blend in.

Not all expressions were named after a person. Some of the words refer, however circuitously, to what they are.

blooch. Chatter, which is what blue jays (the word's origin) sometimes loudly do.

chipmunk. To hoard, or be a hoarder. Think of all the stashing away of winter food that the little four-legged varieties do.

glimmers. Eyeglasses. Eyes are what you get a glimmer in.

Some Boontling words have an innate sense to them once you hear their meaning.

backdated chuck. Someone who's backward or behind the times.

earth. Truth. Think of "down to earth."

Gullah

This Creole language, which developed on the Sea Islands of South Carolina and Georgia, is a melding of English and the West African languages the slaves brought with them in the eighteenth century. The famous Gershwin musical *Porgy and Bess* was based on a novel of Gullah life.

basket name. A nickname in Gullah. Originally, a basket name was given to newborns when they were still in their baby baskets and before they were christened with their formal name. The basket names protected them, should evil spirits try to steal their souls before their christening.

cracking teeth. Talking a lot. Try telling your dentist you've been told you go around cracking your teeth. You'll become his or her walking annuity—until you break the news of what it means. The expression is found in the *Slave Songs of the United States* of 1867. "Crack" is used in the sense of "to open," as when you crack open a door. In this case, it's your mouth (teeth) that you're opening. It also implies that such talk is tiresome, as the expression can be disparaging. Those who crack their teeth too much might try closing their mouths.

day clean. A Gullah expression recorded in the 1867 collection *Slave Songs*, "day clean" can mean dawn or daybreak or full daylight. Before the sun sets on this lovely term and it disappears from the American horizon, let's hope that poets and other writers will adopt it as a fresh way to say that a new day dawns.

Pennsylvania Dutch

Banish all images of tulips and clogs, Gouda and Holland. The Pennsylvania Dutch of southeastern Pennsylvania are not Dutch at all in ancestry. They're German. The German for "German" is *Deutsch*. Americans confused the two words.

The Amish have become synonymous with Pennsylvania Dutch. They are one of several Protestant religious sects who left southern Germany and Switzerland in the late 1600s for the same reason the Puritans hightailed it out of England: religious persecution. William Penn, the Quaker founder of what we know as Pennsylvania, invited them to his neck of the woods. English only became the first language of the Pennsylvania Dutch in the 1850s.

eat yourself done. "Finish eating" in Pennsylvania Dutch parlance. What makes this phrase sound quaint to many ears is the use of the back-atcha pronoun "yourself." (Linguists call it the reflexive pronoun.) *Ess dich satt* is the German translation.

ferhoodled. *Verhuddelt.* Still confused? Ferhoodle = *verhuddelt* = confused, both in the sense of "to be confused" as well as "to confuse matters to the point of messing them up." Such confusion has been around since at least 1872, when "ferhoodled" first made it into print. It looked like this: *Ich bin f'r-huttlt* ("I am confused").

the hurrier I go, the behinder I get. If the Pennsylvania Dutch feel that way in their world of buggy whips, imagine how behinder the rest of us have got in our era of instant messaging. A saying with a similar cadence and immutable logic: **too soon old, too late smart**.

it's making down. If Pennsylvania Dutch had its own Weather Channel, you might hear "it's making rain down" or just "it's making down." It's rather like the way some of us would say "it's coming down" when there's a rain- or snowstorm.

my off is on. Outta here, in Pennsylvania Dutch parlance. When you're *on* vacation, you're taking time *off*, right? Invert the *on* and the *off*, and your off just went on.

Bumfoozled, Bumfuzzled, Bumfuddled

And You Thought You Were Confused

Those who bamboozle (deceive) are often the cause of others becoming **bumfoozled** (confused). Or **bumfuddled** or **bumfoodled** in North Carolina and Kentucky. Or **bumfuzzled** in the Ozarks and Kentucky again. In Nebraska they may know it as being **bumswizzled**. In Virginia they know they've been hoodwinked when they've been **honeyfuggled**. Westerners branded their own brand of being bamboozled back in the early 1800s. They called it **hornswoggled**.

Not to be outdone, Yiddish offers some colorful ways of its own to be confused. Drawing from the German for confused, *verdutzt*, in Yiddish you might be **fartutst**. This can happen when things are **tsedreyt**, all turned and twisted, leaving you **tsetumlt**—which practically has "tumult" written all over it.

outen the light. Turn out the light, Pennsylvania Dutch style. The expression was heard as early as 1878, when it would have meant extinguish the candlelight. In parts of Wisconsin, particularly around Oshkosh, some of the older German stock still outen the light.

smearcase. *Schmierkäse*. Got it? That's German for smear cheese, which made its appearance in print in the 1820s. This "smear" is a little like the Yiddish *schmear*—or *schmeer*, to take it closer back to its German—of cream cheese to spread on the bagel. Smear cheese is a spreadable cheese, like cottage cheese.

the smearcase is all. All what, you ask? All gone.

NAME THE FEATURED CREATURE

Can you guess what this creature is? It's been called a skeeter hawk, a darning needle, a snake feeder, a spindle. An ear sewer, a needle, a snake doctor, a stinger.

In much of the South, especially along the coast of states like North Carolina, you're apt to hear **MOSQUITO HAWK** or **SKEETER HAWK**, perhaps in the hopes that it will eat all those skeeters and their stingers. (In Chicago, this creature *is* the **STINGER**, at least in name.) But in the western part of North Carolina, as well as in the middle part of the country, it's a SNAKE FEEDER or SNAKE DOCTOR. Legend has it that it would stitch up snakes that got injured.

The sewing imagery gains traction as you head north and west, where this creature becomes alternately a DARNING NEEDLE, a DARNER, or a NEEDLE. In the Delaware Valley and coastal New Jersey, they put a different spin on the sewing reference, calling it the SPINDLE.

In the Outer Banks, they call it as they see it: CRANE FLY.

On occasion it's been a DEVIL'S DARNING NEEDLE, for those who feared it would sew up their toes or their lips when they were asleep. The imagery gets even more extreme as you push into Nevada and California. Here the creature is the EAR SEWER. Ouch.

Just what is this creature of many names? The dragonfly.

It's ironic that this delicate-winged insect has been pelted with so many barbed descriptions, given that the dragonfly has long been a symbol of transformation in Christian faiths. Thus you can find dragonflies embedded in stained-glass windows of churches and printed on pages of religious books as a symbol of Christ. An illuminated manuscript that Catholic priests used in the sixteenth century contains a page where a dragonfly represents the cross.

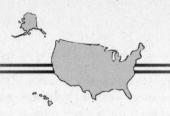

EPILOGUE

Where You Been?

As you've cruised through this book, you may have noticed that a good portion of the conversation has been devoted to the origins of these words. That, of course, is by design. Nothing tells us where we've come from quite like knowing how we got there.

Several origins prove to be obscure, a few are still being debated, and some others are just simply a mystery. This is what happens when people use their language, day after day, generation upon generation. Ask someone why he or she uses an expression and you'll often hear, "I don't know why. I just know I've always said that." It's another way of saying that we use our language in these idiosyncratic and often funny ways because these are the ways that work for us.

That's a good reason. In fact, it's wicked good.

BIBLIOGRAPHY

WEB

"And Just What Is Regular Coffee?" 2 Blowhards. www.2blow
hards.com/archives/2006/08/and_just_what_i_1.html.

Appalachian Regional Commission. www.arc.gov/index.do?
nodeId=2.

Arizona State Visitors Guide 2009. www.arizonastatevisitorsguide
.com/arizona_guest_ranches.html.

Ask a New Yorker. www.askanewyorker.com.

Bowers, Andy. "What's a Boston Brahmin?" *Slate*, March 1, 2004.
www.slate.com/id/2096401.

A Brief History of Coffee and Coffee Timeline. 2BaSnob. www
.2basnob.com/coffee-history.html.

Brown, Robbie. "A Southern Twist: Tea-Infused Vodka." *New
York Times*, February 10, 2009. www.nytimes.com/2009/02/11/
dining/11vodka.html.

Burke Museum of Natural History and Culture, University of
Washington. www.washington.edu/burkemuseum/collections/
paleontology/marine/clams.php.

City-Data. www.city-data.com/states.

City Dictionary. www.citydictionary.com.

City of Boston. www.cityofboston.gov.

CoalSpeak. www.coalregion.com/home.htm.

"Cracker Farmhouses, 1840–1920." Old House Web. www.old
houseweb.com/architecture-and-design/cracker-farm
houses-1840-1920.shtml.

A Dictionary of Earth Sciences. Edited by Ailsa Allaby and Michael Allaby. www.encyclopedia.com/A+Dictionary+of+Earth+Sciences/publications.aspx?pageNumber=1

DJ's Texas State of Mind. http://mstexan7.tripod.com/id3/html.

"Do You Speak American? Track That Word!" MacNeil/Lehrer Productions. www.pbs.org/speak/words/trackthatword.

Double-Tongued Dictionary. www.doubletongued.org.

Encarta World English Dictionary. North American edition. Microsoft, 2009. http://encarta.msn.com.

Epicurious. www.epicurious.com.

Eye of Hawaii. www.eyeofhawaii.com/Pidgin/pidgin.htm.

Federal Writers' Project, Works Projects Administration. Tennessee: A Guide to the State. State of Tennessee: Department of Conservation, Division of Information, 1939. New Deal Network hypertext edition, 1996. http://newdeal.feri.org/guides/tnguide/cont.htm.

FoodReference.com. www.foodreference.com.

The Free Dictionary by Farlex. http://thefreedictionary.com.

H.O. Beer Car Collectors. www.hobeercars.com.

Honorable Order of Kentucky Colonels. http://kycolonels.org.

Kentucky Fried Chicken. www.kfc.com/about/colonel.asp.

Klineman, Jeffrey. "I Wish I Lived in a Land of Lipton." Slate, August 8, 2007. www.slate.com/id/2171917.

Leo, Arnold. "350 Years of Inshore Fishing." East Hampton Star, November 5, 1998. www.easthamptonstar.com/DNN/Archive/1998/981105/hist1.htm.

Liberman, Mark. "Ultimate Toolies." Language Log, August 27, 2005. http://itre.cis.upenn.edu/~myl/languagelog.

Malachite's Big Hole. http://home.att.net/~mman/Glossary.htm.

Merriam-Webster Online Dictionary. www.merriam-webster.com.

Missouri State University, Ozarks Studies Institute. http://ozarksstudies.missouristate.edu.

Murakami, Kery. "SLUT—Streetcar's Unfortunate Acronym Seems Here to Stay." Seattle P-I, September 18 and 20, 2007. www.seattlepi.com/local/332081_slut18.html.

The Nibble. www.thenibble.com.

North Pole West Cowboy Lingo. www.northpolewest.com/Cowboy_Lingo.html.

Norwegian American Homepage. www.lawzone.com/half-nor/nor-am.htm.

Old West Slang. www.rustedfables.com.

Online Dictionary. http://onlinedictionary.datasegment.com.

Online Etymology Dictionary. Edited by Douglas Harper. http://etymonline.com.

Open Source Shakespeare. www.opensourceshakespeare.org.

"Osage orange." Great Plains Nature Center. www.gpnc.org/osage.htm.

OUP Blog, Oxford University Press USA. http://blog.oup.com.

The Phrase Finder. www.phrases.org.uk.

A Prairie Home Companion with Garrison Keillor: Post to the Host. www.publicradio.org/columns/prairiehome/posthost.

Quinion, Michael. "World Wide Words: Michael Quinion Writes on International English from a Dictionary Viewpoint." www.worldwidewords.org.

Roadside America. www.roadsideamerica.com.

Samworth, Herbert. "John Eliot and America's First Bible." SolaScriptura. www.solagroup.org/articles/historyofthebible/hotb 0005.html.

Shotgun's Home of the American Civil War. www.civilwarhome.com/battlenames.htm.

"Sockeye Salmon." National Geographic. http://animals.nationalgeographic.com/animals/fish/sockeye-salmon.html.

Stradley, Linda. "History of Iced Tea and Sweet Tea." What's Cooking America. http://whatscookingamerica.net/History/IcedTeaHistory.htm.

Taggart, Chuck. A Lexicon of New Orleans Terminology and Speech. www.gumbopages.com/yatspeak.html.

Tesro Iron Dog. www.irondog.org.

Texas Almanac. www.texasalmanac.com.

University of Notre Dame College of Arts and Letters. http://al.nd.edu.

Urban Dictionary. www.urbandictionary.com.

Vail, Sharon. "Sourdough: More Than a Bread." National Public Radio, September 13, 2006. www.npr.org/templates/story/story.php?storyId=6061648.

Vintage Vocabulary. www.vintage-vocabulary.com.

A Way with Words. www.waywordradio.org.

Weaver, Eric. The Michigan Accent Pronunciation Guide. www
.michigannative.com/ma_wordsphrases.shtml.

Wicked Good Guide to Boston English. Universal Hub. www
.universalhub.com/glossary.

Wikipedia. http://en.wikipedia.org.

Wisconsin Cheese Curds. Wisconsin Milk Marketing Board.
www.eatcurds.com.

Word Origins. www.wordorigins.org.

Wordsmith.org. http://wordsmith.org.

Yonan, Joe. "Don't Call It a Hot Dog." *Boston Globe*, August 2,
2006. www.boston.com/travel/explorene/rhodeisland/articles/
2006/08/06/dont_call_it_a_hot_dog.

YourDictionary.com. www.yourdictionary.com.

PRINT

Adams, Raymond F. *A Dictionary of the American West*. Norman: University of Oklahoma Press, 1975.

The Alaska Almanac: Facts About Alaska, 30th anniversary ed.
Nancy Gates, ed. Portland, Ore.: Graphic Arts Center Publishing, 2006.

Allen, Irving Lewis. *The City in Slang: New York Life and Popular Speech*. New York: Oxford University Press, 1995.

Almond, Jordon. *Dictionary of Word Origins: A History of the Words, Expressions and Clichés We Use*. New York: Citadel Press, 2000.

The American Heritage Dictionary. 4th ed. Joseph P. Pickett, ed.
New York: Bantam Dell, 2004.

Amory, Cleveland. *The Proper Bostonians*. Orleans, Mass.: Parnassus Imprints, 1947.

Austin, Jane G. *Nantucket Scraps: Being the Experiences of an Off-Islander, In Season and Out of Season, Among a Passing People*. Boston: James R. Osgood, 1883.

Blevins, Winfred. *Dictionary of the American West: Over 5,000 Terms and Expressions from AARIGAA! to ZOPILOTE*. Seattle: Sasquatch Books, 2001.

Blount, Roy, Jr. *Alphabet Juice.* New York: Farrar, Straus and Giroux, 2008.

Bragg, Melvyn. *The Adventure of English: The Bibliography of a Language.* London: Hodder Headline, 2004.

Colt, George Howe. *The Big House: A Century in the Life of an American Summer Home.* New York: Scribner, 2003.

Da Kine Dictionary: Da Hawai'i Community Pidgin Dictionary Projeck. Lee A. Tonouchi, ed. Honolulu: Bess Press, 2005.

Dictionary of American Regional English. 4 vols. to date. Frederic G. Cassidy, chief ed. Cambridge, Mass., and London: Harvard University Press, Belknap Press, 1985–.

Dingus, Anne. *More Texas Sayings Than You Can Shake a Stick At.* Houston, Tex.: Gulf Publishing, 1996.

Doogan, Mike, ed. *How to Speak Alaskan.* Kenmore, Wash.: Epicenter Press, 1993.

Douglas-Lithgow, Robert Alexander. *Nantucket: A History.* New York and London: G.P. Putnam's Sons, 1914.

Dozier, Ray. *The Oklahoma Football Encyclopedia.* Champaign, Ill.: Sports Publishing, 2005.

Flexner, Stuart Berg. *I Hear America Talking: An Illustrated Treasury of American Words and Phrases.* New York: Van Nostrand Reinhold, 1976.

———. *Listening to America: An Illustrated History of Words and Phrases from Our Lively and Splendid Past.* New York: Simon and Schuster, 1982.

Gould, John. *Maine Lingo: Boiled Owls, Billdads and Wazzats.* Camden, Maine: Down East Magazine, 1975.

Hendrickson, Robert. *The Facts on File Dictionary of American Regionalisms.* New York: Facts on File, 2000.

King, Ross. Foreword to *The Grimani Breviary, A.D. 1520.* Delray Beach, Fla.: Levenger Press, 2007.

Lynch, Jack. *The Lexicographer's Dilemma: The Evolution of "Proper" English, from Shakespeare to South Park.* New York: Walker, 2009.

MacNeil, Robert, and William Cran. *Do You Speak American?* New York: Nan A. Talese/Doubleday, 2005.

Mariani, John F. *The Dictionary of American Food and Drink.* New York: Hearst Books, 1994.

McClane, A. J., ed. *McClane's New Standard Fishing Encyclopedia: An International Angling Guide*. New York: Holt, Rinehart and Winston, 1974.

McCool, Sam. *How to Speak Bostonian*. N.p.: Hayford Press, 1985.

McCrum, Robert, William Cran, and Robert MacNeil. *The Story of English*. New York: Viking, 1986.

Metcalf, Allan. *How We Talk: American Regional English Today*. Boston: Houghton Mifflin, 2000.

Mordock, John, and Myron Korach. *Common Phrases and Where They Come From*. Guilford, Conn.: Lyons Press, 2001.

The New Partridge Dictionary of Slang and Unconventional English. Tom Dalzell and Terry Victor, eds. New York: Routledge, 2006.

Nickerson, Joshua Atkins II. *Days to Remember: A Chatham Native Recalls Life on Cape Cod since the Turn of the Century*. Chatham, Mass.: Chatham Historical Society, 1988.

Philips, David E. *Legendary Connecticut: Traditional Tales from the Nutmeg State*. Willimantic, Conn.: Curbstone Press, 1995.

The Random House Dictionary of the English Language, college ed. Laurence Urdang, ed. New York: Random House, 1968.

Rosten, Leo. *The Joys of Yiddish*. New York: McGraw-Hill, 1968.

———. *The New Joys of Yiddish*. Updated ed. New York: Crown, 2001.

Stern, Jane, and Michael Stern. "The Best Hot Dogs in America." *Parade*, May 30, 2010.

Success with Words: A Guide to the American Language. Pleasantville, N.Y.: Reader's Digest Association, 1983.

Thoreau, Henry David. *Cape Cod*. 1865. New York: Penguin Books, 1987.

Tortorello, Michael. "Between Sidewalk and Street, Hope." *New York Times*, May 27, 2010.

Webster, Noah. *A Compendious Dictionary of the English Language: A Facsimile of the First (1806) Edition*. N.p.: Bounty Books, 1970.

Webster's Word Histories. Frederick C. Mish, ed. Springfield, Mass.: Merriam-Webster, 1989.

Wolfram, Walt, and Natalie Schilling-Estes. *Hoi Toide on the Outer Banks: The Story of the Ocracoke Brogue*. Chapel Hill: University of North Carolina Press, 1997.

Wolfram, Walt, and Ben Ward, eds. *American Voices: How Dialects Differ from Coast to Coast*. Malden, Mass.: Blackwell Publishing, 2006.

Wright, John D. *The Language of the Civil War*. Portsmouth, N.H.: Greenwood, 2001.

CONTRIBUTORS

My thanks to all those who lent me their ears, scratched their heads, and shook loose those sayings they thought everyone said.

Victoria Amos
Carol Anderson
James Andrews
John Armato
Karen Aro
Joe Aud
Carmen Ayala
Alicia Biskup
Eric Blinderman
Jamie Brinegar
Brooke Burgess
Krista Carlson
Cindi Carter
Sheila Chambers
Pat Clark
Lisa Smith Coleman
Vicki Landes Cribrari

Rod Danz

Edward Downs

Bruce Dunbar

Katie Feiereisel

Karen Agron Flattery

Larry Ford

Eileen Forde

Cecily Fuller

Karen Funari

Sharon and Steve Graham

Eric Granger

Karen Granger

Xiomara Schwerert Gray

Nancy Green

Maire Griffin

Andrew Hambleton

Lynn McDowell Harmon

Tracey Harrison

Janet Hearn

Ericka Helmick

Robert Hittel

Robert A. Hittel

Suzanne Hogan

Ann Hopka

Edie and Kurt Hoppe

Holly Ites

Lynne Ittleman

Matt Johnson

Clarmarie Keenan

Rita Keiser

Christopher Kellogg

Bill Kern

Melody Kimmel

Jenna Kirkwood

Krista Klaus

Shawn Klein

Gindy and Bill Knoblauch

Hannah Knoblauch

Jennifer LaFlamme

Ian Langworth

Richard Langworth

Dawn Larkin

Mercedes Lawry

Jamie Leicht

Steve Leveen

Claribel Linderman

Faith Linsky

Beth Lodal

Jim Maloney

Sonny McCoy

Harold Glen McPherson

Terry Medaris

Kathryn Messier

Jane Miner

Brittany Mohr

Erik Moses

Robert Nelson

Linda Odell

Laura Parker

Sherri Weiss Poall

Carolyn Quinlan

Ann Wycoff Raab

Mark Rifkin
Paul Saffo
Anna Marie Salas
Jamille Adams Sanford
Christine Schunk
Therese Clements Searle
Jeff Simon
Steve Slaman
Craig Smith
Jessica Smith
Vanessa Smith
Rick Sparkes
Andrea Syverson
Bonnie Syverson
Denise Tedaldi
Karen van Westering
Carole Waller
Shannon Marmion Watts
Raymond A. White
Ann Wylie

MORE THANKS

Many thanks to Ellen Scordato and Alison Fargis of the Stonesong Press, and to Meg Leder of Perigee, for another rewarding collaboration. This could get to be a habit, and I dearly hope it does.

A number of kind souls connected me with contributors or pointed me to helpful sources. I'm grateful to John Armato, Jim Bowie, Kristin Currier, Karen Granger, Adam Grant, Ross King, Lee Klein, Dee Moustakas, Gene Pokorny, Rick Sparkes, and Andrea Syverson for their support and generosity.

Alicia Biskup, Ed Downs, and James Andrews were early readers. Their insights and suggestions helped the book immeasurably.

As always, I owe a huge debt to my mother, Martha Guson, for her cheerleading no matter how arcane the topic I brought up. Who else would have had such enthusiasm for our conversations about smearcase and spiders?

And finally, my thanks to Jennifer and Bill, and to Joe and Dale, for the special language of friendship they speak. It's wicked wonderful.

INDEX

ABOUT THE AUTHOR

Mim Harrison has been eavesdropping on English ever since she spent a year in England and her American ears wondered what language the locals were speaking. She is the author of *Smart Words* and *Words at Work* and the founding editor of Levenger Press, a specialty publisher that has celebrated some of the famous words of Winston Churchill, Samuel Johnson, and Henry David Thoreau. "English is a challenging language to master," she says. "Anyone who attempts it deserves to have some fun with it." She describes the country's regionalisms as "America's oral neighborhoods." She welcomes words from fellow language lovers, who are invited to visit http://mimharrison.com and comment on her blog.